Rolling Stone

THE
100
GREATEST
A L B U M S
OF THE
80S

D1537229

M A R Y   A S T A D O U R I A N : *Project Manager*

D E B R A   B I S H O P : *Book Design*

S U S A N   C O L E : *Production Manager*

Illustration by Terry Allen

Library of Congress Cataloging-in-Publication-Data

Rolling Stone The 100 Greatest Albums of the 80's

     p. cm.
    ISBN 0-312-05148-4
    1. Rock music — 1971-1980 — Discography. 2. Rock music — 1981-1990 —
    Discography. I. Rolling Stone. II. Title: Rolling Stone The One Hundred Greatest Albums
    of the 80's. III. Title: Rolling Stone 100 Greatest Albums of the 80's.
    ML156.5.R6R64 1990
    016.78166'0266 — dc20   90-36109
                                                                 CIP
                                                             MN

First Edition

10   9   8   7   6   5   4   3   2   1

Rolling Stone

THE
100
GREATEST
ALBUMS
OF THE
80S

EDITED BY FRED GOODMAN AND PARKE PUTERBAUGH

FOREWORD BY VERNON REID

ST. MARTIN'S PRESS / ROLLING STONE PRESS • NEW YORK

The Top 100

1. LONDON CALLING   The Clash

2. PURPLE RAIN
   Prince and the Revolution

3. THE JOSHUA TREE   U2

4. REMAIN IN LIGHT   Talking Heads

5. GRACELAND   Paul Simon

6. BORN IN THE U.S.A. Bruce Springsteen

7. THRILLER   Michael Jackson

8. MURMUR   R.E.M.

9. SHOOT OUT THE LIGHTS
   Richard and Linda Thompson

10. TRACY CHAPMAN   Tracy Chapman

11. GET HAPPY!!
    Elvis Costello and the Attractions

12. IT TAKES A NATION OF MILLIONS TO
    HOLD US BACK   Public Enemy

13. DIESEL AND DUST   Midnight Oil

14. SO   Peter Gabriel

15. LET IT BE   The Replacements

16. 1999   Prince

17. SYNCHRONICITY   The Police

18. DIRTY MIND   Prince

19. NEW YORK   Lou Reed

20. PRETENDERS   Pretenders

21. RAIN DOGS   Tom Waits

22. THE SMITHS   The Smiths

23. RED   Black Uhuru

24. LOS ANGELES   X

25. TUNNEL OF LOVE Bruce Springsteen

26. BACK IN BLACK   AC/DC

27. APPETITE FOR DESTRUCTION
    Guns n' Roses

28. CONTROL   Janet Jackson

29. DOUBLE FANTASY
    John Lennon and Yoko Ono

30. HOW WILL THE WOLF SURVIVE?
    Los Lobos

31. AVALON   Roxy Music

32. UH-HUH   John Cougar Mellencamp

33. ZEN ARCADE   Hüsker Dü

34. TATTOO YOU   The Rolling Stones

35. KILL 'EM ALL   Metallica

36. RAPTURE   Anita Baker

37. MIDNIGHT LOVE Marvin Gaye

38. IMPERIAL BEDROOM
    Elvis Costello and the Attractions

39. ELIMINATOR   ZZ Top

40. WAR   U2

41. DOCUMENT   R.E.M.

42. STRONG PERSUADER
    The Robert Cray Band

43. NEBRASKA   Bruce Springsteen

44. OH MERCY   Bob Dylan

45. DAYDREAM NATION   Sonic Youth

46. PETER GABRIEL   Peter Gabriel

47. PRIVATE DANCER   Tina Turner

48. SKYLARKING   XTC

49. CRAZY RHYTHMS   The Feelies

50. MADONNA   Madonna

51. RUN-D.M.C.   Run-D.M.C.

52. MAKING MOVIES   Dire Straits

53. BRING THE FAMILY   John Hiatt

54. SPEAKING IN TONGUES
    Talking Heads

55. CENTERFIELD   John Fogerty

56. CLOSER   Joy Division

57. EMPTY GLASS   Pete Townshend

58. THE INDESTRUCTIBLE BEAT
    OF SOWETO   Various Artists

59. COMPUTER GAMES   George Clinton

60. THE BLUE MASK   Lou Reed

61. DOC AT THE RADAR STATION
    Captain Beefheart
    and the Magic Band

62. PYROMANIA   Def Leppard

63. ENTERTAINMENT!   Gang of Four

64. VIVID   Living Colour

65. IN MY TRIBE   10,000 Maniacs

66. FIYO ON THE BAYOU
    The Neville Brothers

67. TROUBLE IN PARADISE
    Randy Newman

68. THE SPECIALS   The Specials

69. RADIO   L.L. Cool J

70. TRAVELING WILBURYS VOLUME I
    The Traveling Wilburys

71. CROWDED HOUSE   Crowded House

72. MARSHALL CRENSHAW
    Marshall Crenshaw

73. BUILDING THE PERFECT BEAST
    Don Henley

74. SIGN O' THE TIMES   Prince

75. SHE'S SO UNUSUAL   Cyndi Lauper

76. SECOND IMAGE   Public Image Ltd.

77. ROBBIE ROBERTSON
    Robbie Robertson

78. DARE   The Human League

79. GUITAR TOWN   Steve Earle

80. SUZANNE VEGA   Suzanne Vega

81. 1984   Van Halen

82. EAST SIDE STORY   Squeeze

83. LET'S DANCE   David Bowie

84. FAITH   George Michael

85. FREEDOM   Neil Young

86. THE RIVER   Bruce Springsteen

87. STEEL WHEELS   The Rolling Stones

88. LIVES IN THE BALANCE   Jackson Browne

89. WHO'S ZOOMIN' WHO?
    Aretha Franklin

90. . . . NOTHING LIKE THE SUN   Sting

91. LYLE LOVETT   Lyle Lovett

92. FULL MOON FEVER
    Tom Petty

93. THE NIGHT I FELL IN LOVE
    Luther Vandross

94. POWER, CORRUPTION & LIES
    New Order

95. SCARECROW
    John Cougar Mellencamp

96. COLOUR BY NUMBERS
    Culture Club

97. THE MONA LISA'S SISTER
    Graham Parker

98. LABOUR OF LOVE   UB40

99. WHAT UP, DOG?   Was (Not Was)

100. SUN CITY
     Artists United Against Apartheid

Foreword

BY VERNON REID

THERE WAS A REVOLUTION IN MUSIC in the Eighties but it didn't go the way that people expected.

To a large extent, the revolution in music paralleled the Reagan revolution: Radio formats became more corporate and programmers much more conservative in terms of what they were willing to play. The music itself became a tool in quite a revolutionary way – even the song "Revolution" was used to sell sneakers.

I believe that part of the idealism in rock died with John Lennon and Marvin Gaye. For me, the combination of those two deaths was really numbing. I always had a certain idea of music being above and apart and away from the madness of twentieth-century life. But after the Eighties, you couldn't fool yourself into thinking that anymore.

The lyric controversy in which we're now embroiled underscores that fact. Music by bands like Public Enemy and Guns n' Roses could not exist above and beyond and completely apart from life. Conservatism – and not any economic benefits – was really what trickled down from the Reagan revolution. Those values really affected us, creating a climate where record censorship and the labeling of records could even exist. I think that was our revolution in the Eighties.

Fortunately, as this book shows, there were real musical advances in the Eighties. Like everyone else, I have my own list of the Top 100 albums of the Eighties (I would have included both Fishbone and Bad Brains), but the list herein does offer a fair picture of how diverse the music of the last ten years has been.

For me, the biggest musical advances of the Eighties came from the heavy-metal, hip-hop and alternative-rock scenes. It's tempting to think of heavy metal as a white-male subculture within rock & roll; it's almost a rite of passage to be into metal bands. But there's still something there. The hardcore metal scene, which melded punk and what was up until then traditional metal, was very subversive. Bands like the Bad Brains, Black Flag, Anthrax and Megadeth represented a real departure for metal in terms of subject matter – it wasn't just "Let's go party and get wasted." And the fact that Metallica's . . . *And Justice for All* hit Number Six on the Billboard chart within a month of its release speaks volumes of the genre's impact.

The success of Guns n' Roses also says a lot about where kids are at today. The band is a real departure from the blow-dried, made-up bands that have dominated metal in recent years. And there's something vaguely dangerous about the band, drawing audiences to it the way they were previously drawn to Jim Morrison or John Lennon or Morrissey of the Smiths.

The alternative scene brought us a lot of great music, and it also brought us artists who were willing to stand up for rock & roll. When Jello Biafra had to stand trial on obscenity charges because of the *Frankenchrist* cover, it became a rallying point for a lot of people. Even though all charges were dropped, the fight put Biafra's career in shambles.

Similarly, Bob Geldof, who organized Band Aid, really wound up sacrificing his career in a very selfless way in order to see justice done on a larger scale. This decade saw rock artists aligned with many admirable causes, from Farm Aid to Amnesty International. Those concerns were mirrored in the music. An artist like Madonna, who has been actively involved in AIDS benefit work, proved by decade's end to have a lot more substance than many people thought.

When you look at this book and see artists like R.E.M. and Tracy Chapman, you know that the alternative-music scene is alive. It's strange to mention such different artists in the same breath, but it shows the scope of rock's reach during the decade. Even among the most popular artists, the diversity is staggering: In a way Bruce Springsteen was the great American Everyman and Prince was the great American Other Man.

Take a look at how different the top albums in this book are: We start out with the Number One album – the Clash's *London Calling*, a summation of the late-Seventies English punk movement – and we jump an entire world of musical and emotional experience in just going to the Number Two album, Prince's *Purple Rain*. The Top Ten also includes the Talking Heads' influential *Remain in Light*, Bruce Springsteen's *Born in the U.S.A.*, U2's *Joshua Tree*, Michael Jackson's *Thriller*, Paul Simon's *Graceland*, R.E.M.'s *Murmur*, Tracy Chapman's great debut, and Richard and Linda Thompson's underrated *Shoot Out the Lights*.

We don't have to read too far down the list before coming to Public Enemy's *It Takes a Nation of Millions to Hold Us Back*, which crystalizes one man's commitment and rage over African-American life in the latter half of the decade and explodes music conventions in much the same way that Sly Stone's *There's a Riot Goin' On* did nearly twenty years before. And the inclusion of artists like Peter Gabriel, Sonic Youth and Elvis Costello only confirm the richness of music that people managed to create.

If I *had* to pick the singular artist for the decade, it would be Prince. Whatever Prince was doing, we were checking it out. Prince was able to maintain his own fascination with music and his beliefs and his obsessions, and his contradictions are the stuff of which lasting artists are made. He was able to go in several directions at once and wasn't afraid to completely revamp his style and image from one album to the next. The Prince that did *Purple Rain* is certainly not the Prince that did *Sign o' the Times*.

Part of the power of the artists on this list is that their music is not above and beyond what was happening in the streets. It's obvious with a group like Public Enemy, but we shouldn't ignore the fact that a folk artist like Suzanne Vega was able to craft something insidious with a seemingly straightforward song like "Luka," a powerful statement about the kid that you see going to school with a black eye.

The artists on this list aren't just telling stories about survivors – some of them are survivors themselves. That's why Tina Turner's *Private Dancer* is such a powerful record. With the help of some friends, the strength of her convictions gave her the ability to rise like a phoenix; her comeback was one of the most inspiring events of the decade.

Several of the hip-hop and rap albums on this list, like L.L. Cool J's *Radio* and Run-D.M.C.'s debut, show that the current street music owes less to previously existing ideas of rock. From my vantage point as a musician, it is a very real revolution in that the actual means of creating music – utilizing preexisting music through sampling and scratching – is different. It's almost analogous to bioengineering, where you take cells to create other forms of life.

Technology has always had a tremendous effect on popular music. We can go back to the Thirties and Charlie Christian, who is credited with popularizing the electric guitar. He wasn't actually the first to record on the instrument, but through the force of his playing and the visibility he received with Benny Goodman's group, he changed it from a novelty into a viable option for making music. From that, everything else flows: the Scotty Moores, the Chuck Berrys, the Mike Bloomfields, the Jimi Hendrixes, the John McLaughlins. All of that flowed from that option, to the point where the guitar eventually supplanted the piano as the driving force in rock & roll.

Now, here we are in the Nineties, and the technology and ideas of a new generation of musicians are once again reshaping the music. Hip-hop was conceived in a completely organic way by DJs spinning records at parties. They discovered that they could manipulate records in such a way to produce rhythmic sounds akin to a *queeka*, or pressure drum, that could be added to the music already playing on the other turntable.

It was amazing to go to a party where a DJ like Afrika Bambaataa was spinning. He heard all of this music – punk, funk, hip-hop and R&B – as one music. The first thing guys like Bambaataa heard was the beat. It didn't matter what genre a record was, it was cool as long as it had the beat. I remember being interviewed once with Daddy-O of Stetsasonic, and he had all these records with him that you would

never have thought he would have, like Grand Funk Railroad. But they were important to him, and part of that is the democracy of the beat.

Although much of the Eighties' best hip-hop wasn't embraced by the mass media, it still had a tremendous impact. Back in the Seventies, Richard Pryor's records became a mainstream phenomenon even though those records could not be played anywhere. You still had an underground network of people that knew all the routines and were completely into him, and he managed to cross over in a completely underground environment.

The real trouble for hip-hop began when it crossed over. The issue of "rap violence" and the outcry against groups like Public Enemy and 2 Live Crew only came when the records started to become popular and have an impact on the American cultural scene. It's pretty easy to draw parallels between the war being waged now against rap and the kind of resistance that greeted the early rock & rollers of the Fifties. To paraphrase Pete Townshend, it's not for us to judge the music that's being made in the streets – we just have to get out of the way.

For me, it's the seeds of another revolution, one that I feel a part of: reinvesting rock with some of its pluralism. With the rising specter of censorship, one of the hot issues facing us is how free is the music going to be? Although I feel black music has been

under de facto censorship for years, the notion of wholesale censorship of music is still frightening. The real danger is in allowing legislators to control the way American youth grows up and the way it listens to the music. It's really far beyond not wanting people to talk about sex. It's about choice.

If music in the Eighties was forced to deal with the Reagan revolution, then the Nineties will be the countdown decade – the decade of decision. And the music will have to reflect that. I believe that there are people who are disturbed that there are Living Colour albums in their homes. So for me, it's a definite and personal threat, one which will effect the continuation of rock.

Everything has it's season, and that might be tough for a lot of people to accept. Kids have always been looking for an alternative to what their parents listen to – that's the history of rock & roll. The music helps us get through everything; a lot of its power is the catharsis it offers us. Even in the Reagan era, we could be uplifted by a song like Talking Heads' "Life During Wartime" or the Clash's "Rock the Casbah" or Prince's "Let's Go Crazy." Songs like those really helped to point a way out. I know that's what got me through the Eighties. ❧

Vernon Reid is the guitarist and founder of the band Living Colour.

Preface

BY DAVID FRICKE

THIS HAS BEEN THE FIRST ROCK & roll decade without a revolution, or true revolutionaries, to call its own. The Fifties witnessed nothing less than the birth of the music. The Sixties were rocked by Beatlemania, Motown, Phil Spector, psychedelia and Bob Dylan. The Seventies gave rise to David Bowie, Bruce Springsteen, heavy metal, punk and New Wave.

In comparison, the Eighties have been the decade of, among other things, synth pop, Michael Jackson, the compact disc, Sixties reunion tours, the Beastie Boys and a lot more heavy metal. But if the past ten years haven't exactly been the stuff of revolution, they have been a critical time of reassessment and reconstruction.

Musicians and audiences alike have struggled to come to terms with rock's parameters and possibilities, its emotional resonance and often dormant social consciousness. The following survey of the 100 Best Albums of the Eighties, as selected by the editors of ROLLING STONE, shows that the music and the values it stands for have been richer for the struggle. Punks got older and more articulate in their frustration and rage, while many veteran artists responded to that movement's challenge with their most vital work in years. And rap transformed the face – and voice – of popular music.

The first ten entries here span the Clash's polyglot punk, Prince's crossover funkadelica, Afro-bop from Talking Heads and Paul Simon and hymns of innocence and experience by U2 and Tracy Chapman. Further down the list, old-timers like Dylan, the Stones and Lou Reed hit new highs; Public Enemy and Run-D.M.C. kicked out some serious streetwise jams; Metallica and Guns n' Roses established new hard-rock beachheads; and Hüsker Dü, Sonic Youth and the Replacements offered definitive statements of postpunk angst. The embarrassment of riches on this list is all the more remarkable since arthritic radio programming, corporate sponsorship and outbursts of racism and sexism in rap and metal have complicated rock's present and raised fears for its future.

Best-of lists such as this one are by nature subjective. But rock in the Eighties was like that – lively, varied, contentious and, to some degree, inconclusive. Looking at the best rock has had to offer in the Eighties, it's clear that there's plenty of life left in the old beast yet. The next revolution may be just around the corner. ❧

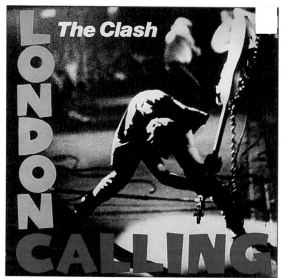

1

LONDON CALLING
The Clash
Epic

Producer: *Guy Stevens*
Released: *January 1980*
Highest chart position: *27*

THIS ALBUM COULD NOT HAVE COME at a more perfect time or from a more appropriate band than the Clash. Released stateside in January 1980, with the decade but a pup and the new year in gear, *London Calling* was an emergency broadcast from rock's Last Angry Band, serving notice that Armageddon was nigh, Western society was rotten at the core, and rock & roll needed a good boot in the rear. Kicking and screaming across a nineteen-song double album, skidding between ska, reggae, R&B, third-world music, power pop and full-tilt punk, the Clash stormed the gates of rock convention and single-handedly set the agenda – musically, politically and emotionally – for the decade to come.

The band had already chalked up two masterpieces of petulant punk fury with *The Clash* (its 1977 debut) and *Give 'Em Enough Rope*. But this time singer-guitarist-songwriters Joe Strummer and Mick Jones fine-tuned the Clash worldview with a deeper sensitivity, addressing issues by zooming in on individuals and hard realities. While the LP's cosmopolitan sound anticipated the world-music fad, its message – revolution begins at home – triggered the reemergence of pop's social consciousness in the Eighties.

For Strummer, Jones, bassist Paul Simonon and drummer Nicky "Topper" Headon, home was London, where they rehearsed and recorded the bulk of the LP during the late spring and summer of 1979 and where there was ample evidence of impending apocalypse (racial tension, rising unemployment, rampant drug addiction). Strummer's catalog of disasters in the title track, scored with Jones's guitar firepower, sets the tone for the record. But that fear and urgency was also very real to the band, which had just split with manager Bernie Rhodes, was heavily in debt and had declared open warfare on the music business.

"I remember that things were so up in the air, and there was quite a good feeling of us against the world," says Strummer. "We felt that we were struggling, about to slide down a slope or something, grasping with our fingernails.

And that there was nobody to help us."

Isolation and desperation are recurring themes on *London Calling*. The Phil Spector-like glow of "The Card Cheat" belies its lyric pathos, while "Hateful" looks at drug addiction from an addict's point of view ("I'm so grateful to be nowhere"). "There was a sense that life really is a succession of heavy blows," says Jones, "that this is what we have to take day to day." Indeed, "Lost in the Supermarket," a dark slice of peppy Euro-pop, was based on Jones's personal life at the time. "I was living in a council flat with my grandmother," he says. "I couldn't get settled. I was supposed to be this rock star, but I was living with my grandmother." Jones and Strummer wrote a lot of songs in his grandmother's flat before Jones eventually moved out.

The album also has fighting spirit to spare in the likes of "Clampdown" ("Let fury have the hour, anger can be power") and "The Guns of Brixton," a Paul Simonon song that combines images of the racially tense Brixton area of London with the outlaw ethic of *The Harder They Come*. "Spanish Bombs," initially inspired by a radio news report of a terrorist bombing in the Mediterranean, evokes the rebellious spirit of the Spanish Civil War.

London Calling became a double album simply because of the energetic rate at which Strummer and Jones were writing songs. "Joe, once he learned how to type, would bang the lyrics out at a high rate of good stuff," says Jones. "Then

I'd be able to bang out some music while he was hitting the typewriter." The members of the Clash devoted nearly three months to arranging and demoing the material at their rehearsal space, a garage in London's Pimlico section, before going into the studio. They added a few choice covers that reflected their widening field of musical vision, such as "Brand New Cadillac," by the British rockabilly legend Vince Taylor, and "Wrong 'Em Boyo," a "Stagger Lee" takeoff by a Jamaican ska group, the Rulers.

The Clash found the perfect produc-

er in Guy Stevens, a kindred renegade spirit with impeccable credentials (he ran the U.K. branch of Sue Records in the Sixties) and an intuitive, if lunatic, genius for getting the *essence* of rock & roll on record. His protégés included Free and Mott the Hoople, and he'd produced the Clash's first demos in 1976. He'd fallen from grace in the industry, but the Clash felt he was just the madman to do the job.

"We sensed it was a good way to keep it on the beam, keep our feet on the ground," Strummer says. "I think something dies in the music when everything is so strait-laced, with accountants monitoring every move."

There was nothing strait-laced about Stevens's methods, which included pour-

ing beer into a piano when the band wanted to use it on a song over his objections and slinging chairs around "if he thought a track needed zapping up," according to Strummer. Stevens nearly hit Jones with a ladder during one take.

But Jones says Stevens – who has since died – was a "real vibe merchant" and was always "exhorting us to make it *more*, to increase the intensity, to lay the energy on."

"Train in Vain," the album's surprise hit, was recorded so late in the sessions that there wasn't time to include it on the cover or label copy. And there is no train in the song, either. "The track was like a train rhythm," says Jones, who wrote most of it, "and it was, once again, that feeling of being lost. So there it was."

Strangely, the Clash was slagged at home for softening up and selling out to mainstream American tastes. "When I read that, the notion was so new to me I just laughed," Strummer says. "In that dirty room in Pimlico, with one light and filthy carpet on the walls for soundproofing, that had been the furthest thought from our minds."

In fact, the Clash was simply showing its punk constituency, and the pop world at large, that there was more than one way to rock the house. The cover design of *London Calling*, a takeoff on Elvis Presley's first album with a photo of Paul Simonon destroying his bass onstage in New York, says it all: This is an album of classic rock & roll values with renewed spirit for a new age. ❧

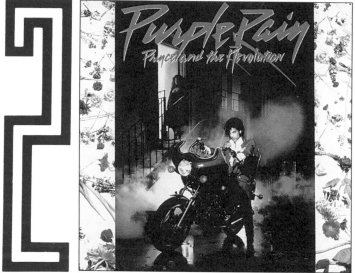

cess was due to its integrity as a cohesive group of striking songs that worked independent of the film. Of his eleven albums released to date, *Purple Rain* stands as the most consistent and accessible album that Prince has yet recorded; it is also his most commercially successful work, selling 14 million copies worldwide. Every track, from the manic rock & roll opener, "Let's Go Crazy," to the moody, inspirational, Beatlesque finale, "Purple Rain," is right on the money. This was Prince's great pop album. "He was a hot artist coming out of the underground," says David Z, an engineer and producer who worked on *Purple Rain*. "Every song was like a single."

In fact, *Purple Rain* contained five hit singles, including "When Doves Cry," his first chart topper, "Let's Go Crazy," which also went to Number One, and "Purple Rain," which reached Number Two.

Purple Rain was the first Prince album to prominently feature his band the Revolution, which played on nearly all the tracks. Recording took place at four locations over the course of a year. Songs were recorded at 1st Avenue, the Minneapolis club featured in the film; the Warehouse, a real warehouse used by Prince for band

PURPLE RAIN
Prince and the Revolution
Warner Bros.

Producers: *Prince
and the Revolution*
Released: *June 1984*
Highest chart position: *1*

'PURPLE RAIN' WAS GOING TO BE Prince's breakthrough album – and he knew it. "Prince was pretty pumped up," says Susan Rogers, who engineered much of the album. "He was ecstatic when he finished it. He was so happy. He knew this was going to be *it*."

Released in tandem with the film, *Purple Rain* was more than simply a soundtrack, and it stands as Prince's most cohesive and accessible album. "He envisioned the film as he made the album," says Alan Leeds, vice-president of Paisley Park Records, Prince's label. "He had a vision before he got in front of the cameras, and he wrote the music to that vision."

While all the songs were included in the movie, the album's runaway suc-

rehearsals; Prince's home studio; and Sunset Sound, in Los Angeles. "The band jelled when Wendy joined [prior to recording *Purple Rain*]," says Bobby Z. "It fell together as a band, and Prince felt like he was one of us. Everything we were doing was getting across better. We were recording and writing and doing it. Even if it was his song, we all worked hard together and did this music together. All of us were in the soup."

Some of the album's success – and certainly its reception by rock and Top Forty radio – was possible because Prince mostly played down the X-rated lyrics and overt sexuality of previous records. There was only one controversial lyric on the album, the much quoted line – "I met her in a hotel lobby/Masturbating with a magazine" – which appears in "Darling Nikki." Ironically, it was that song which prompted Tipper Gore, the wife of Senator Albert Gore, to form the Parents' Music Resource Center (PMRC), the group that lobbied for the placement of warning labels on albums.

Despite the commercial success of *Purple Rain*, Prince's music is innovative and unpredictable, and the album never resorts to pop conventions. "He brought together his influences – the Beatles, Hendrix, George Clinton – and stirred them up," says Leeds. "The real Prince began to pop out. That album

heralded the coming of Prince as an artist-producer-writer. That was the first opportunity to really see Prince the artist fully blossom into his own."

"Let's Go Crazy" was orignally cut live at the Warehouse as the ten-minute version that showed up later on a twelve-inch single. The quirky first single off the album, "When Doves Cry," originally had a more conventional sound. But Prince stripped the song down to its current form, completely removing the bass part. Despite initial qualms among some of the people at Warner Bros.

about the unusual instrumentation, the record was released and quickly reached Number One on the pop charts. "Every once in a while a song comes along that you just know will work for pop radio," says Leeds. " 'When Doves Cry' didn't sound like anything else on the radio."

According to Rogers, "The Beautiful Ones" was Prince's favorite. "He worked the melody out on the piano," she says. "That song meant a lot to him. It was a *big* song for him. It was written for Susannah Melvoin [Prince's girlfriend at the time]. A lot of songs were written about her. That was the first one."

Prince debuted a lot of the

material that would end up on *Purple Rain* during a performance in August 1983 at 1st Avenue. The show was recorded, although Prince didn't initially intend to use the live performances on his album. "I remember people didn't clap because they hadn't heard the songs before," says David Z. "He played all his future hits before them, and they didn't respond."

When Prince heard the tape, he thought it had "the right feel" and decided to use some of the tracks on the album. Ironically, Prince and the Revolution lip-synced their parts for the film's live-performance sequences.

The album's title was something that came to Prince "in a dream," according to Rogers. When Prince first played a version of "Purple Rain" for some of his staff, it caused quite a commotion. "Big Chick [Prince's bodyguard at the time] came into the office raving," says Leeds. "He said, 'Wait until you hear the song he did last night. It's gonna be bigger than Willie Nelson.' "

For Prince, the international success of *Purple Rain* was simply the culmination of many years of hard work, coupled with a strong sense of self-confidence. "I wish people would understand that I always thought I was *bad*," he told a ROLLING STONE reporter in 1985. "I wouldn't have got into the business if I didn't think I was bad." ❧

THE JOSHUA TREE
U2
Island

Producers: *Daniel Lanois and Brian Eno*
Released: *March 1987*
Highest chart position: *1*

BONO WANTED TO EXPLORE ROCK & roll's American roots; the Edge wanted to continue the expressionistic experimentalism of *The Unforgettable Fire*. The creative tensions between them resulted in U2's best record, a multifaceted, musically mature work. "Two ideas were followed simultaneously," says the Edge. "They collided, and this record was born."

The Joshua Tree is the rather esoterically titled album he's referring to — a title that even the typically solemn Bono could joke about. As the U2 singer said to ROLLING STONE's Anthony DeCurtis at the time of its release, "You get record-industry people saying, 'As big as the Beatles — what's the name of the album?' '*The Joshua Tree.*' 'Oh, yeah, oh, right.' It's not exactly *Born in the Joshua Tree*, or *Dark Side of the Joshua Tree*. It sounds like it would sell about three copies."

In fact, the album sold about 12 million copies worldwide, and launched the already popular Irish quartet into the rock stratosphere. But more important than the mass appeal of the album was its message of spiritual and creative yearning, articulated in songs like "I Still Haven't Found What I'm Looking For," "With You or Without You" and "Where the Streets Have No Name." Equally significant was the group's continued examination of political and social issues. In "Running to Stand Still," Bono describes the havoc that heroin use can cause, while "Bullet the Blue Sky" captures the horror and moral outrage that the singer felt about U.S. involvement in Central American politics.

"I just think the album takes you somewhere," says bassist Adam Clayton. "It's like a journey. You start in the desert, come swooping down in Central America. Running for your life. It takes me somewhere, and hopefully it does that for everyone else."

The Joshua Tree is "an album of contrasts," says the Edge. "Bono had fairly strong ideas. He'd been taken with American literature and music. Lyrically, he wanted to follow the blues and get into America. I'd written off white blues in 1978. I was trying desperately to figure out ways to play without using white blues. I wanted to push the European atmospherics. But listening to Robert Johnson and other early blues, I could see what was there. I warmed to the idea."

Both Brian Eno and Daniel Lanois, who coproduced the album, made major contributions. "Brian strongly suggested that we do it all ourselves," says the Edge. "We felt inclined to bring people into the sessions – at times it would have been nice to have pedal steel or background vocals. But he always felt we could do it. There was a great wisdom in that decision."

There was no attempt to make *The Joshua Tree* a commercial album. "If anyone had even *breathed* that idea . . . ," says Clayton. "We wanted to make music. The thing is to challenge radio. To get 'With You or Without You' on the radio is pretty good. You don't expect to hear it on there – maybe in a church."

Before recording began, the group spent time rehearsing at Clayton's house in Dublin, and the atmosphere was so comfortable that they decided to record there. "Just this big, high room," he says. "One of the biggest rooms I've ever seen in a house. With windows and natural light. Pretty much all of it was recorded at my house." The band spent about three months on the album, interrupting the sessions to headline Amnesty International's Conspiracy of Hope Tour in the U.S. Some recording was also done at Dublin's Windmill Lane Studios, at the Edge's house and at another Dublin studio, S.T.S.

Approximately seventeen songs were worked on. Some of the material that didn't end up on the album – such as "The Sweetest Thing," "Spanish Eyes" and "Deep in the Heart" – became B sides of singles.

Lanois credits Eno with sparking many of the music's more adventurous moments. "They had found the experimental side of working on *The Unforgettable Fire* tiring," says Lanois. "But if you work with Brian, like it or not, he's gonna weird things up."

Yet the sessions often had a relaxed, off-the-cuff feel. Of "Running to Stand Still," the Edge says it was "almost improvised to tape." And "I Still Haven't Found What I'm Looking For" originally had a different melody and was called "Under the Weather."

One of the album's best tracks, "Where the Streets Have No Name," proved extremely difficult to record. At one point Eno became so disillusioned with it that he tried to destroy the tape; the engineer told the Edge, "I just had to stop Brian from erasing 'Streets.' "

"It took forever to get that track," says Lanois. "We had this giant blackboard with the arrangement written on it. I felt like a science professor, conducting them. To get the rise and fall, the song's dynamic, took a long time."

Does the band consider *The Joshua Tree* one of the best albums of the Eighties? "With *Joshua Tree*, we wanted to make a really great record, with really great songs," says the Edge. "We became interested in songs again. We put abstract ideas in a more focused form. It's the first album where I really felt Bono was getting where he was aiming with the lyrics. Bono is more of a poet than a lyricist. With *Joshua Tree*, he managed, without sacrificing the depth of his words, to get what he wanted to say into a three- or four-minute song."

"Important?" muses Clayton. "I don't know. It was important for *us*. Suddenly we could do so many different things musically. It gave us a great freedom. I think we were able to stretch and do things we didn't really understand before. It captured a musicality for us that we'd never gotten on record before." ❧

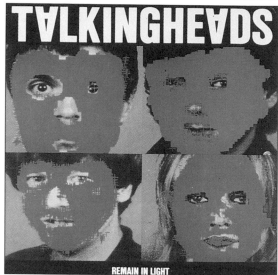

REMAIN IN LIGHT
Talking Heads
Sire

Producer: *Brian Eno*
Released: *October 1980*
Highest chart position: *19*

"A LOT OF PEOPLE DON'T REALIZE THIS, but *Remain in Light* was the worst-selling Talking Heads record ever," says drummer Chris Frantz.

"Financially, we took a beating on that one," says David Byrne. "At the time, it was a really hard sell. The reaction that we heard was that it sounded too black for white radio and too white for black radio."

Remain in Light may have been a commercial disappointment, but musically, the band's 1980 album – which combines funk, disco and African rhythms – was years ahead of its time. "It got great critical acclaim, and we felt that it kind of took popular music to the next phase,"

says Frantz, "which is what we always wanted to do."

But getting there wasn't easy. Depending on who you speak to, tensions in the studio often ran high between at least two parties. "*Remain in Light* was a difficult album to make," says Frantz. "We wanted to do something groundbreaking, but we didn't want to get into fights about it. And a couple of times we did get into fights – *musical* fights – because somebody wanted to go one way and another person thought it shouldn't sound like that."

Within the first week of recording with producer Brian Eno at the Compass Point studios, in the Bahamas, British engineer Rhett Davies quit in frustration. "He said, 'You guys could be making a great pop album,' " says Frantz. "The British, you know, have these ideas about 'great pop albums.' So he left." In his place, they hired David Jerden, who had worked with Eno and Byrne on their recent collaboration, *My Life in the Bush of Ghosts*.

Bassist Tina Weymouth says recruiting Eno was difficult because he and Byrne had had a falling out. "Brian didn't even stay to finish *Bush of Ghosts*," she says. "Something happened between him and David. We asked him to work on *Remain in Light*, and at first he was reluctant. I really don't know what went down between them."

Byrne has slightly different memories of who was fighting whom. "That was between me and Tina," he says with a laugh. "I think she was understandably upset that Brian and I were pushing this whole direction so adamantly. It was almost like it was a train out of control or something. Maybe she felt that she wasn't a part of that. She *was* a part of it, but I can understand how she might have felt." Did that tension affect the album? "Nah," says Byrne, "it was all kind of extracurricular."

Even today, the band members disagree about what they'd set out to accomplish. "We were really intrigued and excited by the formal aspects of African music – the way it was created and put together," says Byrne.

Weymouth, however, says, "David had such a completely different theory about it. His theory was far more intellectual and bookish. I never felt that there was any conscious, manipulative effort on our part to play African styles. To me and Chris, it seemed as if that importance was attached to the record *after* the fact."

While working on *My Life in the Bush of Ghosts*, Byrne and Eno studied voodoo and Afro-Atlantic cultures. "They were very keen on some literature they'd been reading," says Weymouth. "I suppose we all were quite aware of African music

sometime before that. But no one discussed with us the fact we were going to be playing in an African style. To us, it was all very funny, putting this bibliography together with a record. It's so pseudo intellectual and everything we were trying to get away from."

While the music may or may not owe a formal, conscious debt to African styles, the words are definitely more playful than intellectual. Byrne says that Eno encouraged him to be a bit freer with his lyrics. "I really played around a lot more," he says.

"It was the beginning of David finding a way to improvise very quickly in the studio," says Weymouth. "Before, it had been a very private kind of struggle."

For "Crosseyed and Painless," Weymouth says, Byrne was struggling to come up with a vocal part. "Chris had just played drums on the new Kurtis Blow record, 'The Breaks,' which was a real front-runner hip-hop record," she says. Frantz played Blow's album for everyone, and after hearing it, Byrne came up with such lyrics as "Facts are simple and facts are straight/Facts are lazy and facts are late." "It was that whole rap thing," says Weymouth, "but in his own style."

Weymouth claims that most of the

songs on *Remain in Light* came about from jams, yet only Byrne and Eno receive songwriting credits. "Eno called up David and said, 'I really think this is unfair,' " she says. " 'I really think I did more work, and so I think you and I should get all of the credit.' "

That didn't go over well with the rest of the band. "Poor David got yelled at by a lot of people as a result," Weymouth says with a laugh. "But Brian and David were really into this credit thing, I guess."

The album cover, which features computer images over the faces of each band member, was conceived of by Frantz and Weymouth, who'd been experimenting on computers at MIT. "The masks could have been anything," says Weymouth. "They could have been African, they could have been tomatoes on our face. It wasn't really that important – it was just kind of raising questions. Making people think, 'What are they trying to do?'

"We really didn't know. We don't always know what we're doing. We often just get excited, put something down and say, 'Oh, neat.' " ❧

GRACELAND
Paul Simon
Warner Bros.

Producer: *Paul Simon*
Released: *August 1986*
Highest chart position: *3*

FEW ALBUMS HAVE HAD HUMBLER beginnings, been as musically adventurous, generated as much political controversy or been as warmly received by the public as Paul Simon's *Graceland*. Released in 1986, *Graceland* matched Simon with a host of African artists – including guitarist Ray Phiri and his band, Stimela, and the vocal group Ladysmith Black Mambazo. The album's scintillating blend of lively beats and thoughtful lyrics, as well as its seamless fusion of the familiar and the exotic, restored Simon's career and brought African music, and particularly South African music, to a broader international audience.

The journey to *Graceland* began with an unlabeled cassette tape that guitarist Heidi Berg gave to Simon, who listened to it incessantly, without knowing what it was, throughout the summer of 1984. Simon's curiosity eventually got the better of him, and he discovered that the album on the tape was called *Gumboots: Accordion Jive Hits, Volume II* and had been recorded by the Boyoyo Boys, a group from South Africa.

The kind of music on *Gumboots* is *mbaqanga*, or "township jive," the street music of Soweto, South Africa, but for Simon the album called to mind music that was closer to home. "It sounded like very early rock & roll to me – black, urban, mid-Fifties rock & roll, like the great Atlantic tracks from that period," Simon told ROLLING STONE after the album's release. "The rhythm was a fairly up-tempo, 2/4 feel with a strange accordion in there. But the way they play the accordion, it sounds like a big reed instrument. It could almost be a sax."

The music, which seemed to Simon both fresh and reminiscent of the earliest music he loved, suggested a potential new direction for his work. He got in touch with South African producer Hilton Rosenthal, who sent him about twenty additional albums by local musicians, and in February of 1985, Simon traveled to Johannesburg to begin recording *Graceland*. While there, Simon recorded with Tao Ea Matsekha, who helped provide the irresistible groove to "The Boy in the Bubble"; General M.D. Shirinda and the Gaza Sisters, who fired up the funky "I Know What I Know"; and the Boyoyo Boys, who lent the bounce to "Gumboots."

Simon's trip to Johannesburg also triggered a firestorm of protest from antiapartheid groups that charged that, however honorable his intentions may have been, he violated the United Nations cultural boycott of South Africa. For a time it seemed that Simon would be added to the United Nations Special Committee Against Apartheid's list of censured artists — a list that also includes Linda Ronstadt, who sang on "Under African Skies" on *Graceland*.

In the wake of *Graceland*'s release, denunciations flew back and forth. Simon insisted that black South African musicians "voted to let me come," were paid triple the union scale for their work on the album and valued the international exposure *Graceland*

would provide for their music. "To go over and play Sun City, it would be exactly like going over to do a concert in Nazi Germany at the height of the Holocaust," Simon said. "But what I did was to go over essentially and play to the Jews."

The explanation did not wash. "When he goes to South Africa, Paul Simon bows to apartheid," said James Victor Ghebo, the Ghanaian ambassador to the UN and an anti-apartheid activist. "He lives in designated hotels for whites. He spends money the way whites have

made it possible to spend money there. The money he spends goes to look after white society, not to the townships. This is one reason why we do not want people to go there."

Eventually, after months of recriminations, both sides simply seemed to tire of the battle. Simon was never formally added to the list of censured artists. For his part, Simon reluctantly wrote a letter reiterating his refusal to play in South Africa — he had twice previously turned down offers to play Sun City — and donated proceeds from a number of concerts on the *Graceland* tour to black charities in the United States and South Africa.

From Simon's point of view, *Graceland* helped in the struggle to end apartheid. "I never said there were not strong political implications to what I did," he said near the end of the *Graceland* tour. "I just said the music was not overtly political. But the implications of the music certainly are. And I still think it's the most powerful form of politics, more powerful than saying it right on the money, in which case you're usually preaching to the converted. People get attracted to the music, and once they hear what's going on within it, they say, 'What? They're doing *that* to these people?' "

Joseph Shabalala of Ladysmith Black Mambazo tells a story about life in Johannesburg that lends resonance to Simon's defense. "I remember there was a riot there," he says. "People were fighting, the kids were fighting. But not Black Mambazo. The policeman ask us, 'Where do you come from?' I said, 'We come from singing.' They said, 'You are singing while the people are fighting?' I say, 'Yes. They are doing their job. I am doing my job.' " ❧

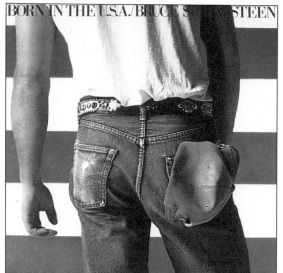

BORN IN THE U.S.A. / BRUCE SPRINGSTEEN

BORN IN THE U.S.A.
Bruce Springsteen
Columbia

Producers: *Bruce Springsteen
Jon Landau, Chuck Plotkin
and Steve Van Zandt*
Released: *June 1984*
Highest chart position: *1*

"I HAD WRITTEN A CATCHY SONG," BRUCE Springsteen recalled in an interview last year with ROLLING STONE, "and I felt it was a really good song, probably one of my best since 'Born to Run.' I knew it was going to catch people – but I didn't know it was going to catch them like *that*, or that it was going to be what it was."

Born in the U.S.A. – the album, the song and the sixteen-month tour – turned out to be the breakthrough that Springsteen fans had been expecting for a decade. The influential Jersey musician became the world's biggest rock star – and a bona fide American icon, to boot.

As a result, Springsteen found himself dominating the album charts in 1984 and 1985. He hit the Top Ten seven times and wound up in heavy rotation in the theretofore unfamiliar terrain of MTV. The album inspired those who knew what his bitter, tough-minded songs were really saying (from numerous songwriters to novelist Bobbie Ann Mason, whose *In Country* owes a debt to the LP), as well as many others who misinterpreted and exploited the cover's American-flag imagery (among them, both 1984 presidential candidates and countless advertising agencies and jingle writers).

For Springsteen, who'd been catapulted into the media spotlight almost ten years previously, when his album *Born to Run* landed him simultaneously on the covers of *Time* and *Newsweek*, *Born in the U.S.A.* afforded him an opportunity to do it over again, older and wiser and not so awestruck by the machinery of fame. "The *Born in the U.S.A.* experience obviously had its frightening moments," Springsteen told ROLLING STONE. "But I was thirty-five, and I had a real solid sense of myself by that time. With *Born in the U.S.A.*, I had a chance to relive my 1975 experience when I was calm and completely prepared and went for it. It was like 'Great. We're selling all those records? Dynamite.'"

Springsteen and the E Street Band had recorded seven of the songs on *Born in the U.S.A.* prior to the release of Springsteen's preceeding album – the stark, neo-solo collection *Nebraska* – in a three-week blitz in May 1982: "Glory Days," "I'm Goin' Down," "I'm on Fire," "Darlington County," "Working on the Highway," "Downbound Train" and – most crucial of all – "Born in the U.S.A."

Springsteen originally recorded the last of these on the acoustic demo tape that became *Nebraska*, but he quickly abandoned that version, feeling it didn't really work in that format. At the start of the May sessions with the full band, Springsteen revived the song in a new, electric arrangement. "Bruce started playing this droning guitar sound," says drummer Max Weinberg. "He threw that lick out to [keyboardists] Roy [Bittan] and Danny [Federici], and the thing just fell together.

"It absolutely grabbed us. We played it again and got an even better groove on it. At the end, as we were stopping, Bruce gave me the high sign to do all these wild fills, and we went back into the song and jammed for about ten minutes, which was edited for about ten minutes, which was edited out. I remember that night as the greatest single experience I've ever had recording, and it set the tone for the whole record."

For a while, though, Springsteen was ambivalent about following through with the rock record whose tone had been so dramatically set by "Born in the U.S.A." "He spent a good deal of time after the release of *Nebraska* feeling very close to that album," says Springsteen's manager, Jon Landau, who coproduced *Born in the U.S.A.* "I don't think he was ready to suddenly switch back into the 'Born in the U.S.A.' mode."

Springsteen drove to Los Angeles, where he began recording demos on his own, most of them closer in sound and spirit to *Nebraska* than to *Born in the U.S.A.* Some, like "Shut Out the Light," eventually appeared as B sides; others, such as "Sugarland" and his overhaul of Elvis Presley's "Follow That Dream," never appeared.

When he returned to recording with the E Street Band, the sessions were marked by prolific songwriting and a freewheeling approach on the part of Springsteen. "I remember one night when we were completely packed up to

go home and Bruce was off in the corner playing his acoustic guitar," says Weinberg. "Suddenly, I guess the bug bit him, and he started writing these rockabilly songs. We'd been recording all night and were dead tired, but they had to open up the cases and set up the equipment so that we could start recording again at five in the morning. That's when we got 'Pink Cadillac,' 'Stand on It' [both used as B sides] and a song called 'TV Movie.' . . . Bruce got on a roll, and when that happens, you just hold on for dear life."

In the end, though, most of the sessions were inconclusive. Of the dozens of songs he recorded from mid-1982 to mid-1983, only "My Hometown" would make *Born in the U.S.A.*'s final cut.

Eventually, Landau and coproducer Chuck Plotkin convinced Springsteen that the best songs were from the May 1982 sessions. Late in the recording process, however, Springsteen wrote a few more standouts, including "Bobby Jean," his benediction to guitarist Steve Van Zandt, who'd left the band to pursue a solo career, and "No Surrender," an optimistic raveup. The album slowly and painstakingly assumed a shape with the help of band members, colleagues and friends who were asked to vote for their favorites from about twenty contenders.

Born in the U.S.A. appeared to be finished, but then Landau, in an exchange that he admits was "testy, by our standards," told Springsteen that the album needed another song. He had a list of requirements: It should unify the record, it should be written in the first person, and it should capture where Bruce was at that point in time. Springsteen objected – "The obvious response is, 'Hey, if that's what you want, then write it yourself,' and I got a little bit of that in this case," says Landau – but three days later Springsteen played Landau a new song born of his frustration and confusion. Its title was "Dancing in the Dark." With that, his blockbuster was finished.

Born in the U.S.A. was Springsteen's triumph, though he doesn't regard it as his best work. "That was a *rock* record," he says from the vantage point of four years later. "When I put it on, that's kind of how it hits me. But I never really felt like I quite got it." ❧

THRILLER
Michael Jackson
Epic

Producer: *Quincy Jones*
Released: *December 1982*
Highest chart position: *1*

WHEN TWENTY-THREE-YEAR-OLD
Michael Jackson and his producer,
Quincy Jones, began recording *Thriller*, they hoped to create a great record that would at least equal the 8
million unit sales of Jackson's prior
solo outing, *Off the Wall*. "No matter
what you do, you are competing
against your previous product and
everybody expects more," Jackson
told a reporter in 1983. What
they ended up with eight months
later became the biggest-selling
album in history.

Thriller, reportedly recorded for
$750,000, has sold more than 40 million copies worldwide – and it still
sells. It earned Jackson over 150 gold
and platinum awards worldwide and a
record seven Grammys. At the
height of Michaelmania in 1984,
Epic Records was selling in excess of 1 million Jackson records *a week*. *Thriller* was the musical equivalent of the Hula-Hoop, an item that *everybody*
had to own.

At the center of all the madness was a slick, entertaining,
endearingly innocent forty-two-and-a-half-minute collection of pure pop music that
produced seven Top Ten singles: "Wanna Be Startin' Somethin'," "The Girl Is Mine,"
"Thriller," "Beat It," "Billie
Jean," "Human Nature" and
"P.Y.T. (Pretty Young
Thing)." "It felt like entering
hyperspace at one point," says
Quincy Jones about the phenomenal success of *Thriller*. "It
almost scared me. I thought,
'Maybe this is going *too* far.'"

With *Thriller*, Jackson and Jones
were aiming for a dynamic, balanced
collection of potential hits. Jackson
supplied many of the best songs on
the album, writing "Wanna Be Startin' Somethin'," "Beat It" and "Billie
Jean" (as well as the slight number
"The Girl Is Mine," a duet with Paul
McCartney). Jones went through
over 300 songs in search of additional material. "I was trying to find a
group of songs that complemented
each other in their diversity," says

Jones. "Give me a ride, give me some goose bumps. If 'Billie Jean' sounds good, it sounds even better followed by 'Human Nature.' 'Wanna Be Startin' Somethin' ' into 'Baby Be Mine.' I look at an album as a total piece."

It began during the spring of 1982 at Michael Jackson's Tudor-style mansion, in Encino, California, where he had been working on material in his sixteen-track studio. Jones and his engineer, Bruce Swedien, spent several days there with Jackson, listening to "Polaroids," their term for the crude demos Jackson had made.

In April they moved to Westlake Audio, in Hollywood, where the majority of the album was recorded. Jones called on a crew of seasoned studio veterans, including guitarist David Williams, drummer Leon Ndugu Chancler, bassist Louis Johnson and percussionist Paulinho Da Costa as well as a number of synthesizer and keyboard players, including Greg Phillinganes, Michael Boddicker, David Foster and Steve Porcaro. The first song cut was "The Girl Is Mine." "Michael and Paul worked very fast," says Swedien. "Three days and it was done."

The album is full of special touches, from Vincent Price's campy introduction to "Thriller" to Eddie Van Halen's raging hard-rock solo on "Beat It." Many of these ideas were Jackson's own. Particularly innovative was the repeated vocal motif – "ma ma se, ma ma sa, ma ma coo sa" – that ends "Wanna Be Startin' Somethin'." "That's based on an African riff from the Cameroon region," says Jones. "Michael came up with it, and we added harmonies and made a whole thing out of it."

Price's "Thriller" rap was written by Rod Temperton during a cab ride to the studio, and Jackson recorded the wolf howls in the alley outside the studio. "I think the idea of 'Thriller'

was to incorporate drama into pop," says Jones of the song, which was originally titled "Starlight Love." "It's like a one-act play."

Jones had to coax Jackson into writing "Beat It." "I bugged him for three months about doing a strong rock thing," said Jones. "Finally he wrote it. I had to squeeze it out of him."

He was also reluctant to do what Jones calls a "beg" on "The Lady in My Life." "That's asking a girl to give you some," says the producer, laughing. "That's against Michael's nature." But at other moments, the singer's enthusiasm was obvious, and he frequently danced as he sang his final vocals – indeed, Jackson's dancing can still be heard in the final mix of "Billie Jean."

Jones and Jackson thought they had the album wrapped in November. They were wrong. "I took Michael home, and he went to sleep on the couch," says Jones. "Three hours later we went back to the studio and listened to the acetate. Biggest piece of shit in life. We were horrified. So we took two days off, then spent the next eight days remixing. One song a day. We put those babies in the pocket."

Thriller has been an extremely influential album. "I hear it a lot in the records produced by Jimmy Jam and Terry Lewis," Jones says. "[Janet Jackson's] 'Funny How Times Flies (When You're Having Fun)' is 'The Lady in My Life.' The new jack swing. Everybody began to understand the power of melody again after *Thriller*."

Perhaps *Thriller*'s biggest accomplishment has been its influence on other black musicians. "It inspired black artists not to look at themselves in a limited way," says Jones. "Before Michael, those kinds of sales had never happened for a black artist. Michael did it. He did it for the first time." ❧

MURMUR
R.E.M.
I.R.S.

Producers: *Mitch Easter and Don Dixon*
Released: *September 1983*
Highest chart position: *136*

"WE WERE CONSCIOUS THAT WE were making a record that really wasn't in step with the times," says R.E.M.'s Peter Buck of *Murmur*, the group's enchanting first album. "It was an old-fashioned record that didn't sound too much like what you heard on the radio. We were expecting the record company to say, 'Sorry, this isn't even a record, it's a demo tape. Go back and do it again.'"

For the most part, I.R.S. Records liked *Murmur* a great deal, and so did an audience that embraced R.E.M. as one of the most significant new bands of the Eighties. From the mysterious photograph of a kudzu-covered train station on the jacket to the intriguingly off-kilter music within, *Murmur* quietly broke with the status quo and mapped out an enigmatic but rewarding new agenda. There is nothing obvious or superficial about R.E.M.'s songs or the way the band chooses to play them. Meanings are hidden in a thicket of nonlinear imagery, with mumbled or distant vocals from Michael Stipe. Elliptical language occasionally jumps out in terse phrases such as "conversation fear" (from "9-9") as *Murmur* bypasses logic and goes straight for the subconscious – a state of altered awareness not unlike the rapid-eye-movement stage of dreaming from which the band took its name.

The members of R.E.M. incorporated elements of folk and country music into pop that was, by turns, bright and murky. Theirs was a quasi-traditional yet boundary-breaking sound that served as a blueprint for alternative bands throughout America for the rest of the decade.

Initially outcasts on the arty-party band scene spawned by the B-52's in their hometown of Athens, Georgia, the members of the group profess to draw more inspiration from Velvet Underground and the Byrds than from any of their contemporaries. They also claim to have learned a lot from Gang of Four and the English

Beat, with whom they toured early on. "They taught us about what a rock & roll band could be, idealistically," says Buck.

Though the individual members weren't extraordinary technical musicians, the balance of personalities within R.E.M. made for a startling chemistry. "It was a unique combination of people, where there was enough tension and enough cohesiveness," says Don Dixon, who produced and engineered *Murmur* with fellow North Carolinian Mitch Easter. "There was a tremendous amount of energy and a lot of real subtle things going on." Buck's rhythmic strumming allowed Mike Mills to play melody lines on the bass and freed drummer Bill Berry from mere timekeeping. Drawing from his fertile imagination, vocalist Stipe launched R.E.M. into a whole other dimension.

The four organized the band in Athens in 1980, traipsing across the South to play anywhere that would have them and cutting one single ("Radio Free Europe") and a five-song EP (*Chronic Town*) at Easter's garage studio in Winston-Salem, North Carolina. For *Murmur* they moved eighty miles south to Charlotte's Reflection Studios, a twenty-four-track facility whose principal client was Jim and Tammy Bakker's PTL Club. (Stipe, in fact, left Charlotte with a souvenir PTL license plate and an autographed Tammy Bakker single.) The group balked at recording elsewhere. "We wanted to do it in the South with people who were fresh at making rock & roll records," says Buck. "In Charlotte we could sit up all night and mess around, have ideas and not worry too much."

R.E.M. had chosen and sequenced the material for *Murmur*, most of which was written in 1980 and 1981, before entering the studio. Producers Easter and Dixon provided technical expertise and offered opinions. "They were instrumental in teaching us how to use

the studio," says Buck. Very little was done by the book. Stipe, for instance, generally recorded his vocals in a darkened stairwell off to the side. Although his vocal approach was unusual for rock, Easter and Dixon had no intention of altering his style. "I was not about to go in and say, 'Oh, Michael, I can't quite understand your line about the placenta falling off the end of your bed,' " says Dixon. "We were dealing with a fragile sort of art concept and trying to bring in a little pop sensibility without beating it up."

If anyone at I.R.S. had reservations about *Murmur*, the band didn't want to know. "The people that heard it were like 'God, this is a really good record, *but . . . ,*' " says Buck. "And we'd go, 'Sorry, see you later.' Because once they start saying *but* and you listen, you're in trouble."

The band added a lot of quirky, experimental touches to the basic tracks in the overdub stage. "We spent most of our time finding interesting ideas and sounds," Buck says, "like laying down ten acoustic guitars, a lot of vocals way low in the mix, strange percussion things, banging on table legs, tearing up shirts. I'd play acoustic guitar and then take the guitar off and leave the reverb on with the delay, so that it was ghostly and strange."

"We did have some rules," says Dixon, "in that if you were going to fly something in backwards or fly in hunks of music triggered off a drum by James Brown, you could only do it one time, and you couldn't go back and try to get something to work." The band members also had talismans, of sorts, to which they became attached: Two plastic dinosaurs purchased by Buck at a Salvation Army thrift shop across the street, marked L for left and R for right, were placed atop the studio speakers. "The reason our records are so good is the dinosaurs," Buck says. "They've been on the speakers for every album we've ever made." ❧

Richard & Linda Thompson

SHOOT OUT THE LIGHTS
Richard and Linda Thompson
Hannibal

Producer: *Joe Boyd*
Released: *June 1982*
Highest chart position: *None*

"EVEN IN THE BEST DAYS OF OUR marriage, Richard and I didn't communicate with each other fabulously well," says Linda Thompson. "I think that the reason the music was good was that we tended to save it for work." Perhaps that explains why *Shoot Out the Lights* is both the best and last album Richard and Linda Thompson made together.

For a change of pace, the Thompsons had decided to record an album with producer Gerry Rafferty, who as an artist had scored a hit with "Baker Street." But Rafferty's slick, elaborate style was at odds with the straightforward way the Thompsons usually recorded, and the kindest thing Richard can say today about the abortive Rafferty record is "I don't think it was wholly successful." Linda, who still has the master tapes in her attic, is more explicit: "Richard hated it."

Enter Richard's friend, producer Joe Boyd, who brought the Thompsons into the studio to cut a quick, low-budget album for his small independent label, Hannibal Records. Richard found himself in more familiar surroundings – he and Boyd had worked together twelve years before, when Richard was the lead guitarist with the pioneering folk-rock group Fairport Convention. Recording was done at Olympic Studios, an old Fairport haunt, with a band that included the Fairport rhythm section of drummer Dave Mattacks, bassist Dave Pegg and guitarist Simon Nicol. Three days into the sessions they had the basic tracks for *Shoot Out the Lights*.

The record turned out to be the soundtrack to what Boyd calls "an elaborate soap opera." Richard's lyrics are crystal-clear portraits of dissolving relationships, cast with wronged or dissatisfied lovers on the one hand and riveting tales of death and violence on the other. There's no concealing the desperation of "Man in Need." Shortly after the record was completed, Richard left Linda, who was pregnant at the time, for another woman.

Richard dismisses the idea that the lyrics presaged what was to happen to their ten-year-old marriage. "The theorists can theorize," he says, "and they may be right, but from a practical point of view, for myself, it was just the stuff I was writing, and it didn't bear any relationship to life as I could see it at the time."

"Do you buy that?" is Linda's disbelieving response. "There was a cohesion to all those songs that was part of what was going on at the time," she says. "We gravitated to that kind of subject matter. There was a kind of common denominator in those songs – they fit together, and we weeded them out that way."

According to Linda, that common denominator was "utter misery. It was kind of a subliminal thing, but that was definitely it," she says. "I think we both were miserable and didn't quite know how to get it out – I think that's why the album is so good. We couldn't talk to each other, so we just did it on the record."

The tension took its toll on Linda's voice. A victim of "studio fever," she developed a nervous tic that made her lose breath, making it difficult for her to keep her voice at full strength for more than a couple of lines at a time. As a result, Boyd was forced to painstakingly stitch together complete vocals from several takes. But for all the studio trickery, the performances have a real cohesion and showcase Linda's achingly beautiful voice.

The poignancy of English folk music is evident in Linda's heartbreaking "Walking on a Wire" and Richard's caustic "Back Street Slide." The latter, the album's hardest rocker, modifies an Anglo-Irish folk melody with an odd-metered, almost Zeppelinesque riff pinched from a tune the guitarist had heard on Algerian radio.

The album's masterpiece, though, is its title track. A slow, dissonant rocker about a psychotic killer, it was, according to Richard, originally about the Russians in Afghanistan. "Somehow it developed into this urban melodrama," he says. "I can't understand how that happened."

On *Shoot Out the Lights*, Richard reclaimed what he calls his "license to rip" and came up with his most inspired and unrestrained guitar playing since the glory days of Fairport Convention. Nowhere is Richard's renaissance more apparent than on the masterful second solo of "Shoot Out the Lights": alternately soaring and

twitching, Thompson's guitar echoes a psychopath's flitting emotions, ending on a tantalizingly unresolved note.

The song nearly didn't make it onto the record. If Richard had had his way, the light pop tune "Living in Luxury" would have been there instead. "It's Richard at his most frivolous," Boyd says of "Living in Luxury." The song was left off the record. (It now appears as a bonus track on the *Shoot Out the Lights* CD.)

At the end of each side is respite – a calm in the eye of the storm. The gentle ballad "Just the Motion" "was an attempt, deliberate or unconscious, to write something that was a bit restful," says Richard. To close the record, the Thompsons duet on the perversely joyous "Wall of Death,"

ostensibly about an amusement-park ride. "You can waste your time on the other rides," they sing, "but this is the nearest to being alive."

The ensuing tour was understandably tense and marked by screaming matches both on and off the stage. "I felt like I really sang great for the first time in years on that tour," says Linda. "It was a release, literally and figuratively."

Despite the string of excellent records that preceded it, *Shoot Out the Lights* remains the Thompsons' most commercially successful effort, even though it never made the pop charts. With more than a trace of bitterness, Richard acknowledges that part of its appeal is the couple's split. "I think it may have helped sales," he says. "It's a great promotional ploy – I recommend it."

And he still doesn't think it's the best thing he and Linda ever did. "I don't understand why people like it particularly. Well, I think the songs are good. But I don't think the performances are outstanding. And we still get complaints about the drum sound, especially from the drummer."

On the other hand, Linda considers *Shoot Out the Lights* to be the couple's best work. "People are often really horrified to hear me say, 'I do wish in a way that I was going through that again,'" she says. "They say, 'But you were mad, demented and ill!' And I say, 'Yeah, but I really could sing good.' So there's always an upswing, even in that darkest moment." ❧

TRACY CHAPMAN
Tracy Chapman
Elektra

Producer: *David Kershenbaum*
Released: *April 1988*
Highest chart position: *1*

"THIS ALBUM WAS MADE FOR THE right reasons," says David Kershenbaum, who produced Tracy Chapman's debut album. "There was a set of ideas that we wanted to communicate, and we felt if we were truthful and loyal to those ideas, then people would pick up on the emotion and the lyrical content that was there." The stark realism of Chapman's songwriting, combined with her warm, richly textured vocals, brought a refreshing integrity to the airwaves.

Chapman was discovered in 1987 by fellow Tufts University student Brian Koppelman. "I was helping organize a boycott protest against apartheid at school, and someone told me there was this great protest singer I should get to play at the rally," says Koppelman, who now works in A&R at Elektra. He went to see Chapman perform at a coffeehouse called Cappuccino. "Tracy walked onstage, and it was like an epiphany," he says. "Her presence, her voice, her songs, her sincerity – it all came across."

Koppelman approached Chapman after the performance and said, "I don't normally do this, but I think my father could help you a lot." (Charles Koppelman, his father, was then co-owner of SBK Publishing, one of the largest independent song publishers in the world.) Chapman listened politely but didn't say much and went on her way.

Undaunted, Koppelman continued attending her shows, sitting in the front row. Although Chapman finally agreed to talk, she declined to cut any demos for him. Then Koppelman found out that Chapman had already recorded some demos at the Tufts radio station, WMFO, for copyright purposes. (In exchange, the station got to broadcast her songs.) Koppelman went to the station, and while a friend distracted the DJ, he lifted one of the tapes. It had one song, "Talkin' Bout a Revolution," on it. He made a copy and took it to his father. "He immediately got the picture and flew up to see her," Koppelman says.

Chapman's demo tape with SBK led to a signing with Elektra. "I have to say that I never thought I would get a contract with a major record label," she told an interviewer shortly after the album's release. "All the time since I was a kid listening to records and the radio, I didn't think there was any indication that record people would find the kind of music that I did marketable. Especially when I was singing songs like 'Talkin' Bout a Revolution' during the Seventies. . . . I didn't see a place for me there."

David Kershenbaum was suggested by an SBK executive, according to Koppelman, after several other producers turned down the project. "I'd been looking for something acoustic to do for some time," says Kershenbaum. "There was a sense in the industry of a slight boredom with everything out there and that people might be willing to listen again to lyrics and to someone who made statements."

Chapman's greatest concern during her meetings with Kershenbaum was that the integrity of her songs remain intact. "She said right off the bat that she wanted the record to be real simple," says Kershenbaum. "I wanted to make sure that she was in front, vocally and thematically, and that everything was built around her."

Every song on the album, with the exception of "Fast Car," was on the SBK demo. Chapman played "Fast Car" for Kershenbaum during their first meeting. "I loved it the minute I heard it," he says. "It was the most heartfelt song on the album, as far as people relating to it and visualizing what the songs were."

Tracy Chapman was recorded over an eight-week period at Powertrax, Kershenbaum's Hollywood studio. As many as thirty different bass players and drummers were invited to come in to play with her. "Mountains o' Things" was the hardest track to cut. "Tracy was so used to just singing and playing that when she got into the slight rhythm changes a band might add, it was somewhat disorienting for her," Kershenbaum says. "We had [percussionist] Paulinho Da Costa in one day, and we tried it with just Tracy and him." That wound up being the version used, with other instruments added later. In a similar way, "Behind the Wall" was recorded a cappella – and left as is.

The album opens with "Talkin' Bout a Revolution," which is "a good introduction to who she is and what she's saying," says Kershenbaum. The running order of the other ten songs on *Tracy Chapman* was determined by writing song titles out on three-by-five cards and shuffling them around in different sequences.

How did the album's success affect the artist? "I didn't get the feeling that she lost her perspective at all," says Kershenbaum. "She's really pretty solid. In fact, if anything, she's gotten much smarter and wiser." ❧

11 GET HAPPY!!
Elvis Costello
and the Attractions
Columbia

Producer: *Nick Lowe*
Released: *March 1980*
Highest chart position: *11*

"WE KNOCKED OFF A FEW GOOD grooves on that one, I suppose," said Elvis Costello of *Get Happy!!* earlier this year. Of course, he understated the case for his fourth album considerably. *Get Happy!!* – on which Costello and the Attractions race through twenty flawless soul-pop gems in just over forty minutes – is perhaps the smartest, most impassioned party record of the decade.

It may also be the most listenable *mea culpa* in rock history.

In the winter of 1979, while in Columbus, Ohio, on tour in support of *Armed Forces*, Costello got involved in an ugly argument with Bonnie Bramlett and members of Stephen Stills's band at a hotel bar. In a misguided effort to offend Bramlett and company, the British New Waver – who had been active in Britain's Rock Against Racism movement – made some racist remarks about black American musicians. The result was a painful and humiliating public-relations disaster for Costello that saw him receive death threats and have his records dropped from radio-station playlists.

While Costello dealt formally with the incident at a press conference in New York City a few days later, he did a much better job of clearing the air with this album, which affirmed his respect and affection for the music of black America. *Get Happy!!* was his and the Attractions' version of a Motown album and therefore an attempt to disprove some false accusations. "I had the feeling people were reading my mind," Costello told ROLLING STONE's Greil Marcus in 1982, "but what could I do, hold up a sign that read, I REALLY LIKE BLACK PEOPLE?"

For *Get Happy!!* Costello and the Attractions – keyboardist Steve Nieve, bassist Bruce Thomas and drummer

Pete Thomas – again worked with producer Nick Lowe, though in a new location, Withlord Studios, in Amsterdam. Lowe came up with a low-tech, back-to-mono sound that suited Costello's soul-revival approach. Many songs were pieced together from notes made during the *Armed Forces* tour. As Tom Carson wrote in a ROLLING STONE review, "This is an album that springs straight from the tensions and interruptions of life on the road – all of its scenes seem to take place in motel rooms or between planes or over long-distance phone lines."

The desperate, bitter romantic longing telegraphed in so many of the album's lyrics is offset by a light touch musically. Though *Get Happy!!* was the product of a difficult, even "demented" (according to Costello) time in his life, there are moments when, lost in the soulful gait of the music, he sounds, well, downright *happy.* ❧

12
IT TAKES A NATION OF MILLIONS TO HOLD US BACK
Public Enemy
Def Jam/Columbia

Producers: *Hank Shocklee and Carl Ryder*
Executive producer: *Rick Rubin*
Released: *July 1988*
Highest chart position: *42*

"I WANTED TO TRY TO MAKE A HIP-HOP version of Marvin Gaye's *What's Goin' On*," says the leader of Public Enemy, Chuck D. "Something that was *there*, something that was a staple, something that no matter how many times you played it, you had to go back to it again and

again." Only time will tell if *It Takes a Nation of Millions to Hold Us Back*, a potent rap discourse on drugs, poverty and black self-determination, will compare with Gaye's eloquent classic of social realism.

After their first album, the members of Public Enemy gained a new social perspective, and these self-proclaimed prophets of rage articulated the anger implicit in the hard beats and bottomless bravado of ghetto-born rap. "Bring the Noise" and "Rebel Without a Pause" blasted out of beat boxes, Jeeps and BMWs all summer; the phrase "Don't believe the hype" became the "Where's the beef?" of 1988; and despite being aimed at urban blacks, the album also won a large white audience.

Virtually every track contains repeated shrill noises that are both irritating and riveting; its agit-rap sound communicates as much rebellion as the lyrics. "Most people were saying that rap music was noise," says producer Hank Shocklee, "and we decided, 'If they think it's noise, then let's show them *noise!* But we're also gonna give them something to think about.'"

Like many sounds on the album, the distinctive dive-bombing squeal of "Rebel Without a Pause" is actually an inspired bit of digital alchemy – a mixture of the JBs and Miles Davis. "We use samples like an artist would use paint," says Shocklee. The album packs literally hundreds of collaged sounds drawn from

more than 150 different recordings. Snippets of speeches by Malcolm X, Louis Farrakhan and Jesse Jackson were also employed.

But the biggest noise came courtesy of Public Enemy's lyrics. "I don't rhyme for the sake of riddlin'," says Chuck D. in "Don't Believe the Hype," as he castigates the media for painting the members of the band as criminals and declares, "I'm not a racist." The chilling "Black Steel in the Hour of Chaos" portrays a convicted draft dodger who leads a violent jailbreak, and "Party for Your Right to Fight" ladles out Black Muslim rhetoric about "grafted devils." For some badly needed comic relief, there's a solo turn by Chuck D.'s foil Flavor Flav, "Cold Lampin' With Flavor," a relentless cascade of hip-hop argot (*lampin'* means "hanging around on the corner by the street lamp").

Some critics complained that Chuck D. spent more time barking than biting

on *It Takes a Nation of Millions*. But in the end, Chuck D. attributes the bravado to the exigencies of making a good rap record. "If I'm working on an album, I've got to drop some *smackin'* rap jams," he says. "I mean, this is *music*, too. If I was a preacher, I would be in a church. I'm trying to do something that hasn't been done before in popular music." ❧

13

DIESEL AND DUST
Midnight Oil
Columbia

Producers: *Warne Livesey and Midnight Oil*
Released: *December 1987*
Highest chart position: *21*

THE NEXT TIME YOU HEAR SOME rock star moaning about life on the road, think of this album and the remarkable tour that inspired it. In the summer of 1986 – which is actually winter down under – the Australian rockers and political activists of Midnight Oil packed amplifiers, sleeping bags and good intentions into a cara-van of four-wheel-drive vehicles and embarked on a concert tour of remote Aboriginal settlements in the Northern Territory.

The members of the band ate grubs and wallaby meat and played on makeshift stages under chilly night skies for audiences huddled around campfires. They also witnessed firsthand the extreme poverty, cultural devastation and spiritual resilience of the island continent's original settlers. The Oils' awe and anger came pouring out in *Diesel and Dust*, an album caked with outback grit and charged with hard-rock moxie and melodic savvy. Contrasting images of Aboriginal desperation and determination with the ruins of white manifest destiny, *Diesel and Dust* is a site-specific document rooted in a basic theme of man's inhumanity to man.

The Oils' odyssey had started a couple of years earlier, when at the request of a teacher friend, they played to 300 Aborigines at a settlement near Darwin. "It made a greater impact on us than playing in New York . . . or to audiences of 30,000 anywhere," lead singer Peter Garrett told an Australian reporter in 1986. "The more we toured overseas, the more the desire grew to get out with the Aborigines and learn more about our own country."

Shortly before the tour, Midnight Oil was commissioned to write a song for a documentary about the return of a sacred tribal site, Ayers Rock – or Uluru, the Aboriginal name – to its rightful owners. The band delivered "The Dead Heart," a song of ghostly urgency that was a Number One hit down under and subsequently became the centerpiece of *Diesel and Dust*. Also written at the same time was "Beds Are Burning," another powerful song about Ayers Rock. Appropriately, the band played both songs for its Aboriginal audiences; at one settlement, Kintore, the village elders responded to the Oils' sincerity by allowing them to participate in a sacred tribal ceremony.

Upon returning to their Sydney home base, the Oils wrote the rest of *Diesel and Dust* and undertook a tour of sweaty local pubs to road-test the material before recording it with British producer Warne Livesey. The resulting album gave the band

its first gold album in America, as well as a Top Twenty single in "Beds Are Burning." It also fulfilled Midnight Oil's longstanding desire, in drummer Rob Hirst's words, "to write Australian music that people overseas could get into and understand, which would enlarge their whole vision of Australia past Vegemite sandwiches and kangaroo hops." ❧

14

SO
Peter Gabriel
Geffen

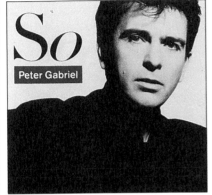

Producers: *Daniel Lanois and Peter Gabriel*
Released: *May 1986*
Highest chart position: *2*

"I WAS THINKING OF DOING A BLUES and soul album," says Peter Gabriel about the origins of *So*, his multiplatinum 1986 album. "I was going to do half existing songs – favorite songs from my teenage years – and half new stuff. 'Sledgehammer' was the first song I developed for that project."

It was also the first single from *So*. Propelled by a powerful groove and a groundbreaking Claymation video, "Sledgehammer" went to Number One, opening the door for the album's commercial success. Daniel Lanois, who coproduced Gabriel's instrumental soundtrack for the film *Birdy* and then was invited back to work on *So*, says he and Gabriel wanted the album to be engaging and accessible.

"We had mutually decided on a philosophy for the record – that we would incorporate a playfulness and a humanness," says Lanois. "I thought it was important for Peter to be very clear with some of these songs. I wanted the listener to be able to touch the voice. I was definitely looking to bring Peter to the foreground."

Despite its mass appeal, however, *So* also presented compelling challenges. "Mercy Street" draws on the work of the influential American poet Anne Sexton, who committed suicide in 1974. Senegalese singer Youssou N'Dour wails a spectacular background vocal on "In Your Eyes." A Depression-era shot by the American photographer Dorothea Lange and Gabriel's concern about the miners on strike in England inspired Gabriel to write "Don't Give Up."

The cartoonish rocker "Big Time" harpoons the excesses of Eighties-style

ambition, while the haunting "We Do What We're Told" derives from a university experiment in which test subjects were asked to administer what they believed were injury-inducing electric shocks to others and complied, in the majority of cases, rather than disobey the authority figure giving them instructions. Addressing Gabriel's recurrent theme of control – "One is ego dominant, and the other is ego submissive," he says – these two songs define extremes that must be avoided.

Given the album's thematic reach, why the seemingly offhand title? "I liked the shape and the fact that it didn't have too much meaning," Gabriel says in his elliptical way. ❧

15 LET IT BE
The Replacements
Twin/Tone Records

Producers: *Steve Fjelstad Paul Westerberg and Peter Jesperson*
Released: *November 1984*
Highest chart position: *None*

AFTER THREE ALBUMS OF endearingly loud, fast rock & roll, the Replacements took a giant step forward without surrendering their raucous edge on *Let It Be*. By then, leader Paul Westerberg had developed into a first-rate songwriter, capable of soul-baring introspection ("Unsatisfied"), wry character studies ("Androgynous") and frenzied, go-for-broke rock ("We're Coming Out"). *Let It Be* caught one of America's most promising bands at an early creative peak, straddling the line between inspired amateurism and accomplished, deliberate craftsmanship.

For Westerberg, *Let It Be* was a break with the Replacements' punk aesthetic. "Playing that kind of noisy, fake hardcore rock was getting us nowhere, and it wasn't a lot of fun," he says. "This was the first time I had songs that we arranged, rather than just banging out riffs and giving them titles." The anthemic opening number, "I Will Dare," was written on acoustic guitar – a first for Westerberg.

Constrained by what people wanted the group to be – the loud, sloppy and lovable Mats, as they were known to fans – Westerberg let his feelings out on *Let It Be* with songs like "Unsatisfied." "I was not terribly happy," admits Westerberg. "It was just the feeling that we're never going anywhere and the music we're playing is not the music I feel and I don't know what to do and I don't know how to express myself. I felt that one to the absolute bone when I did it."

Let It Be, cut at a small Minneapolis studio, Blackberry Way, was the final album in which the Replacements' hell-raising lead guitarist, Bob Stinson, had a key role, and blowouts like "We're Coming Out" were written with him in mind. Stinson was present but not really accounted for on the next studio album, *Tim*, and was out of the band by the time *Pleased to Meet Me* was recorded. His younger brother, Tommy, remains the band's bassist, and Chris Mars the drummer.

The title *Let It Be*, of course, came from the Beatles. Appropriating it, says Westerberg, "was our way of saying that nothing is sacred, that the Beatles were just a damn fine rock & roll band. We seriously were gonna call the next record *Let It Bleed*." The songs on *Let It Be* were cut quickly and crudely. "We didn't have a producer looking over our shoulder,

saying, 'This isn't done, boys,' " Westerberg says. Yet *Let It Be* has a solid emotional core, and the Replacements' evolution was fitting. "The jump from a wild punk band to one that actually plays songs and has some interesting stuff came at the right time," says Westerberg. ☙

16

1999
Prince
Warner Bros.

Producer: *Prince*
Released: *October 1982*
Highest chart position: *9*

RECORDING A TWO-RECORD SET AT A
time when he had yet to become a
major star was a risky thing for
Prince to do – but the risk paid off.

Upon its release, *1999* became
Prince's biggest seller; two singles,
"Little Red Corvette" and "Delirious,"
went Top Ten, while the title track
reached Number Twelve. Although it
contained only eleven songs, clocking in at

nearly seventy minutes, *1999* gave Prince
the room he needed to address some of his
favorite topics: sex, romance, freedom and
even rock critics, who were toyed with in
"All the Critics Love U in New York."

The album is both experimental and
commercial. The title track is a
prime example of Prince's pop
craftsmanship, utilizing multiple
lead vocals; the lyrics – about
dancing in the face of
Armageddon – remain the
perfect metaphor for the
modern age. And the infectious
"Little Red Corvette" leaped
onto pop radio.

"I think he was trying to
become as mainstream as
possible, without having to
compromise any of his ideas,"
says keyboardist Matt Fink,
who was a member of Prince's
band the Revolution at the time. "To some
extent, he was trying to make something
that would be pleasing to the ear of the
average person who listens to the radio, yet
send a message. I mean, '1999' was pretty
different for a message. Not your average
bubblegum hit."

Prince recorded much of the album at
Uptown, his name for the basement studio
he had built in his infamous purple house,
located in a suburb of Minneapolis. The
basement studio was more sophisticated
than the one he had used for *Dirty Mind*
and included a twenty-four-track recorder.
"The groove got settled," says drummer
Bobby Z. "He knew it was back to dance.
There wasn't anymore of the 'Ronnie Talk

to Russia' kind of songs. There was some
weird stuff, like 'Something in the Water,'
but it was still very funky. I think he found
his groove, and the groove never left."

Although only Prince was billed on
1999 – like the three releases that
preceded it – the album portended the
integration of his band into future
recording projects. He shared some of the
lead vocal spots with keyboardist Lisa

Coleman and guitarist Dez Dickerson, and
Dickerson contributed the searing solos on
"Little Red Corvette." On the psychedelic
purple album cover, in small, backward
lettering that partially obscures the *i* in
"Prince" are the words "and the
Revolution." "He was setting the public
up for something that was yet to come,"
says Bobby Z.

Bobby Z. remembers the months
Prince spent on *1999* as a period of intense
creativity, when Prince's credo was
"Anything goes." "A lot of experimental
sound and backwards stuff was tried," says
the drummer. " 'Lady Cab Driver' was
very innovative with the street sounds and
almost a kind of rap. 'Something in the
Water' was definitely using the Linn drum
machine to its fullest. Prince was
experimenting to get to something like the
next album [*Purple Rain*]; *1999* gave him
the keys to a lot of doors." ❧

17

SYNCHRONICITY
The Police
A&M

Producers: *Hugh Padgham and the Police*
Released: *June 1983*
Highest chart position: *1*

THE LAST POLICE ALBUM WAS THE BEST Police album – musically and thematically. *Synchronicity* was as good as thinking man's New Wave ever got. On it, singer, bassist and chief songwriter Sting applied Swiss psychologist Carl Jung's theories of the collective unconsciousness and mystical coincidence (a.k.a. synchronicity) to personal, embittered studies of pain, vengeance and the agony of love's labors lost.

The material was dark but well suited to the group's method of interaction in the studio: "violence," according to Sting in a 1983 interview. "I'll argue till the cows come home about something I believe in, and so will Andy and Stewart," he said, referring to guitarist Andy Summers and drummer Stewart Copeland. "*Synchronicity* went through all kinds of horrendous cogs and gears to come out, emotionally and technically, the way it did."

It was the last album by the fractious Police, who quietly dissolved after a half-hearted and unsuccessful attempt to reunite in the studio three years later. Yet there was little evidence of battle on *Synchronicity*. Sting's bracing tenor was dramatically framed by the subtle third-world inflections in Copeland's drumming and Summers's delicately serrated guitar. The band displayed a refined sense of pop drama in "Every Breath You Take" – a chilling ode to obsession heightened by a haunting guitar riff – and the gothic strains of "King of Pain."

Closer to the surface were Sting's own wounds, suffered during a messy divorce in 1982 from actress Frances Tomelty, his wife of seven years.

sense of pop drama in "Every Breath You Take" – a chilling ode to obsession heightened by a haunting guitar riff – and the gothic strains of "King of Pain."

Closer to the surface were Sting's own wounds, suffered during a messy divorce in 1982 from actress Frances Tomelty, his wife of seven years. Afterward, he went to Jamaica, staying at novelist Ian Fleming's old house and writing a large chunk of *Synchronicity* – including "Every Breath You Take," "King of Pain" and "Wrapped Around Your Finger" – at the same desk Fleming had written his James Bond novels. The recurring images of entrapment and pain in Sting's lyrics dovetailed with his interest in Jungian theory, which he set to music in "Synchronicity I" and "Synchronicity II."

"The title of the album refers to coincidence and things being connected without there being a logical link," he said. Sting has continued to psychoanalyze himself in song as a solo artist, but *Synchronicity* captured him at a particularly vulnerable and eloquent juncture in his career. As he himself said, "I do my best work when I'm in pain and turmoil." ❧

18 DIRTY MIND
Prince
Warner Bros.

Producer: *Prince*
Released: *October 1980*
Highest chart position: *45*

'DIRTY MIND' MARKED PRINCE'S COMING of age. It was the first album on which he successfully synthesized the rock and soul he had grown up on into a vibrant, strikingly original sound, at the same time turning his own sexuality and flamboyance into a clear-cut style and stance. His vocals – including crystal-clear falsettos – established Prince as one of the preeminent pop singers of the Eighties.

If Marvin Gaye had opened the bedroom door a crack nearly a decade earlier with sexually frank songs like "You Sure Love to Ball," Prince ripped that door right off its hinges. *Dirty Mind*'s lyrics cover oral sex ("Head"), incest ("Sister") and a *ménage à trois* gone bad ("When You Were Mine") and set a new standard for mainstream pop music, paving the way for tamer tracks like George Michael's "I Want Your Sex."

Then there is the music: a daring mix of modern technology, raw rock & roll and irresistible funk. Prince's keyboard-dominated "Minneapolis sound" became the blueprint for a generation of soul, funk and pop groups. His influence is evident in songs ranging from Ready for the World's "Oh Sheila" to Fine Young Cannibals' "She Drives Me Crazy."

Working mostly alone in a cramped, makeshift sixteen-track basement studio in his Minneapolis home on Lake Minnetonka, Prince created *Dirty Mind* in a few months. Many of the songs were cut quickly – often in one night. He took engineering credit under the pseudonym Jamie Starr. "Maybe he didn't want it to seem like he did *everything*," says keyboardist Matt Fink, who helped write the album's title track and played on both "Head" and "Do It All Night." About half of the material was written during a tour that found Prince and his band opening for soul star Rick James; Prince whipped up "When

You Were Mine" in a Florida hotel room. "It was probably inspired by an old girlfriend," says Fink.

The title track was based on a jam riff Fink created that Prince took a fancy to when he heard the band playing it one day during rehearsal. "He asked me to come over to his house," says Fink. "I left at 2:00 a.m. after we cut basic tracks. By the next morning he'd finished it."

Although Prince's sexuality was apparent on his first two albums, it came to the forefront on *Dirty Mind*. "He really found himself with that album," says Bobby Z, who was the drummer in Prince's band at the time. "I think he wrote better songs. And the roughness of it gave it an edge – it was a little more garage sounding."

"That really was him at the time," says Fink. "He was rejoicing in his own sexuality. He was saying, 'Sex is a reality, don't be afraid of it.' "

Prince naturally expected the album to

be controversial. "He knew he was entering some hot soup," says Bobby Z. "Any time you do anything where you're pushing the envelope, you know?"

But Prince's father wasn't impressed. "When I first played *Dirty Mind* for him," Prince once said, "he said, 'You're swearing on the record. Why do you have to do that?' And I said, 'Because I swear.' " ❧

19

NEW YORK
Lou Reed
Sire

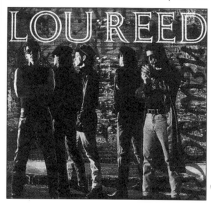

Producers: *Lou Reed and Fred Maher*
Released: *January 1989*
Highest chart position: *10*

"FAULKNER HAD THE SOUTH; JOYCE had Dublin; I've got New York – and the environs," said Lou Reed this past spring, and he was not being immodest. The Big Apple, rotten or otherwise, has been both the setting for and subject of Reed's ongoing novel-in-music since the mid-Sixties, when he penned his first chapters on drugs, sex and desperation in the urban shadows and set them to the primal beat of the Velvet Underground.

But on his 1989 installment, *New York*, Reed took Manhattan and turned it inside out with a vengeance fueled by moral outrage. In a carefully scripted fourteen-song suite, he addressed the plight of the homeless, the hopeless and victims of AIDS and racial prejudice with the same clenched, bristling imagery and acidic wit he'd once applied to the city's uptown glitterati and downtown bohemians.

Reed then scored his libretto for two guitars (Reed and Mike Rathke), bass (Rob Wasserman) and drums (Fred Maher, who coproduced with Reed). The sound of *New York* is rooted in the brute metallic attack of the original Velvets; drummer Maureen Tucker even played on two songs, including the Andy Warhol tribute "Dime Store Mystery."

Except for an occasional overdub, *New York* was recorded live in the studio. Indeed, the false start at the beginning of "Romeo Had Juliette," the album's opening track, is exactly as Reed and crew flubbed it on the first day of recording. "It was the first song I had written," Reed told ROLLING STONE shortly after the album's release. "We went in and did it in a day. And that's the take, the one you hear."

Prior to recording, Reed put the songs through an intense three-month bout of editing and rewriting at his home in New Jersey. "Even before pen hits paper, I really self-edit a lot," he explained. "So when I go to write something, it's pretty close, even just the first draft. But it's way better by the sixth."

When a song started to take shape, Reed would bring in Rathke to play along on guitar, "because I couldn't play

my part and sing at the same time," said Reed. "It was too new. Mike played my guitar part, and I would sing, for real. And where it didn't work, I rewrote it there, rewrote it and rewrote it until every word was exact."

While Reed insisted in *New York*'s liner notes that the album was designed to be listened to in a single sitting, "as though it were a book or a movie," he admitted in conversation that the songs were not sequenced in any particular dramatic order.

"We had tried to put the songs in order, to tell the story moodwise and emotionally," said Reed. "And when it didn't work, it was so bad it was unbelievable. Then Victor [Deyglio], one of the engineers, said, 'There's a trick I've learned over the years. Why not put it in the order that it was recorded in?' And there it was. Wow!" ❧

20

PRETENDERS
Pretenders
Sire

Producer: *Chris Thomas*
Released: *January 1980*
Highest chart position: *9*

"TO SUMMARIZE THE PRETENDERS," says Chrissie Hynde, the band's vocalist, songwriter and founder, "all I can say is that we were the genuine article. In fact, we were so genuine we killed ourselves." She is referring to the drug-related deaths of original band members James Honeyman-Scott and Pete Farndon in the early Eighties. "We never had any pretensions," she continues.

"If it sounded dangerous, it was because it *was* dangerous."

Indeed, on *Pretenders*, the band backs Hynde's potent vocals with fast, aggressive playing. She wastes no time on politeness or protocol; her songs are blunt, hard-nosed treatises on social and sexual politics, such as the dark, carnal "Tattooed Love Boys." A sense of defiant self-worth emerges in the soulful, chugging "Brass in Pocket," in which Hynde sings, "I'm special, so special/ I've got to have some of your attention/Give it to me!"

As Ken Tucker wrote in a ROLLING STONE review, *Pretenders* tells stories "about how good, tempestuous sex can be redemptive; how bad relationships thrive on degrees of contempt; how passionate self-absorption can sometimes open up into a greater understanding of the people with whom you're involved."

By 1980, Hynde – who grew up in Akron, Ohio – had been living in England for the better part of a decade. As a part-time writer for the British music weekly *New Musical Express*, she'd found herself sometimes questioning the validity of that line of work. "In 1973, I realized that there was no point in being a journalist and just knocking everything that was going on at the time," Hynde says. "Then it occurred to me, 'What the hell, why not me?' About 1976, I saw that the moment was coming when I

could get away with it. It's all about timing, you see. If you wait long enough, your number comes up."

She met three musicians from Hereford, near Wales – guitarist Honeyman-Scott, bass player Farndon and drummer Martin Chambers – and they formed the Pretenders. Their music was more diverse than the machine-gun rhythms of punk, because the three Britons were accomplished musicians and Hynde had grown up on a diet of AM radio. "I didn't quite fit into the London punk scene because I'd been listening to too many Bobby Womack albums, you know?" says Hynde. "My musical background was a little too rich for the punk thing."

The Pretenders did share with punk an outsider's contempt for society, however. The debut album was an uncensored expression of the motivations that drew Hynde and the

others to rock & roll in the first place. "I thought being in a band was an antiestablishment lifestyle," she says. "It's only ever been my interest to maintain that, and to maintain my freedom as a bum. I don't want to be recognized; I don't want to be hassled. I just want to play guitar in a rock & roll band." ❧

21
RAIN DOGS
Tom Waits
Island

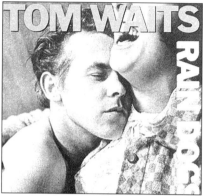

Producer: *Tom Waits*
Released: *August 1985*
Highest chart position: *None*

WITH 'CLOSING TIME,' RELEASED IN 1973, Tom Waits staked out a rock & roll gutter all his own, gruffly crooning beat-poet tales of drifters over R&B and jazz-tinged accompaniment. With the 1983 release *Swordfishtrombones*, his vocals turned more ragged, his songwriting more eclectic and his orchestrations more "junkyard."

His noisome world was never so beautiful as on his tenth album, *Rain Dogs* – his first self-production and the first time he recorded in his new hometown of New York City. The album is "a little more developed and more ethnic feeling," he said at the time. "Kind of an interaction between Appalachia and Nigeria."

The title, Waits said, referred to the fact that "dogs in the rain lose their way home, [because] after it rains, every place they peed on has been washed out. . . . They go to sleep thinking the world is one way, and they wake up and somebody moved the furniture."

The cover photo depicts a prostitute comforting a sailor who looks disconcertingly like Waits. From the first clanking strains of "Singapore" ("We're all as mad as hatters here") to the closing New Orleans-style spiritual "Anywhere I Lay My Head," the nineteen songs on *Rain Dogs* are peopled by such lost souls.

"Tango Till They're Sore" was written about a friend who jumped out of a window; "9th & Hennepin" recalled the time Waits was stuck in the middle of a pimp war at a Minneapolis doughnut shop. But for the most part, while writing songs for *Rain Dogs*, Waits said he "was thinking of the guy going back to Philadelphia from Manhattan on the Metroliner with the *New York Times*, looking out the window in New York as he pulls out of the station, imagining all the terrible things he doesn't have to be a part of."

Despite impressive walk-ons from Keith Richards, Robert Quine and John Lurie, it was the band Waits patched together that bravely follows him down every skanky alley. Guitarist Marc Ribot lent his oddball twang to "Jockey Full of Bourbon" and the title cut; bassist Larry Taylor provided an ominous underpinning; and percussionist Michael Blair filled in the gaps with marimba, bowed saw, parade drum and anything else that wasn't nailed down.

"If I couldn't get the right sound out of the drum set," Waits said, "we'd get a chest of drawers in the bathroom and hit it real hard with a two-by-four." In that way, he explained, "the sounds become your own." ❧

THE SMITHS
The Smiths
Sire

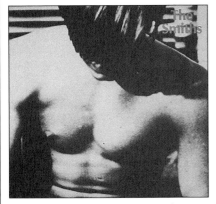

Producer: *John Porter*
Released: *March 1984*
Highest chart position: *150*

WITHOUT THE HELP OF A MAJOR LABEL, a video or any real promotion, the Smiths' 1984 debut entered the U.K. charts at Number Two and became an alternative-radio favorite in the U.S. "We were incredibly sure of ourselves at the time," says guitarist Johnny Marr of himself and singer-lyricist Morrissey.

The band's single "This Charming Man" filled a gap on the radio. "Up until then, either you were a chart group with no substance or you were kind of an indie group who nobody ever got to hear," says Marr. " 'This Charming Man' found a happy compromise. It brought a real commercial sound together with interesting lyrics and a good groove concept."

Morrissey, the brooding lead singer, wrote provocative, literate lyrics to accompany Marr's haunting melodies.

"I went specifically to Morrissey's house because I knew he was a singer and a great writer, and I was desperate to pull a group together," says Marr. "I'd had enough of a bland music scene in England, and I felt like the time was absolutely right for us. On the face of it, it wasn't the most original thing to just get a four-piece band – guitar, bass, drums and a voice – but at the time, there was a move in England towards synthesizer music and duos. And lyrically, no one was dealing with the things that Morrissey was."

The first two songs the pair wrote together (before bassist Andy Rourke and drummer Mike Joyce joined the band) were the melancholic "Hand That Rocks the Cradle" and the bittersweet "Suffer Little Children."

"We just kind of built from there," says Marr. "I'd put all of the stuff on cassette and give it to Morrissey. We wrote so quickly that it didn't take us long to write the entire first LP – four weeks from start to finish. And that kind of kept that intensity up. We had a really close relationship that was really difficult for most people to penetrate."

Although the album was eventually recorded at Manchester's Pluto recording studio, the Smiths originally tried to cut it in London. "We recorded a whole load of tracks in London and it just didn't feel right," says Marr.

The band hooked up with producer John Porter during a Radio One session for the BBC. "We were actually waiting to be produced by somebody else, and John just happened to wander through the studio when we were setting up our equipment. We realized he was ex-Roxy Music and so on, and within about ten minutes of talking to him, we decided to sack the other producer. For me, as a guitarist, it was one of the best things that ever happened. I was starting to develop my style, and he saw something in my playing that he really felt he could work on."

Things were a little more strained between Marr and Morrissey. "There were one or two fights," Marr admits. "We had a very intense relationship. It wasn't exactly a laugh a minute." While the creative friction between Marr and Morrissey propelled them through future albums, that same intensity led to the band's eventual dissolution in 1987. ◈

23
RED
Black Uhuru
Mango

![BLACK UHURU album cover]

Producers: *Sly Dunbar and Robert Shakespeare*
Released: *June 1981*
Highest chart position: *None*

UNTIL THE LATE EIGHTIES, ONLY ONE foreign musical culture, Jamaica's reggae and its antecedent ska, had managed to exert a major influence on rock & roll. With the passing of reggae's primary architect and prophet, Bob Marley, the Kingston-based vocal trio Black Uhuru appeared poised to assume the mantle of reggae's leadership. At a moment when the music was in critical need of a strong new voice, Black Uhuru's finest album, *Red*, shone with all the musical intensity and political fervor of the Rastafarian movement.

Black Uhuru, formed in 1974 by singers Derrick "Duckie" Simpson, Garth Dennis and Don Carlos, took its name from the Swahili word for freedom (*uhuru*) and cut a handful of Jamaican singles that failed to attract much attention. After several lineup changes, Black Uhuru solidified as a trio consisting of Simpson, fellow Kingstonite Michael Rose and American social worker turned performer Sandra "Puma" Jones.

Along the way, Black Uhuru also replaced its original producer, Jamaican dub master Lee "Scratch" Perry, with the bass and drum battery of Robbie Shakespeare and Sly Dunbar. The thunderous drumming of Dunbar and heartbeat bass of Shakespeare were already earning them a reputation as one of the world's finest rhythm sections. Black Uhuru's first collaboration with them – which was also the first recording for Sly and Robbie's Taxi Records label – caught the attention of Island Records president Chris Blackwell (the man who introduced Bob Marley and the Wailers to the world). The group made its debut on Mango/Island in 1980 with *Sensimilla*. On *Red*, released the following year, the propulsive, electronic sound of the band solidified.

Red is a plea for cultural revolution and religious faith. From the opening "Youth of Eglington," a call not to arms but to thought and clean living for Rastafarians, through the closing "Carbine," which counsels patience to Rastas in the diaspora, *Red* strives to send a message of hope to a people in cultural exile. Along the way, Black

Uhuru celebrates the naturalist and nationalist roots of its lifestyle.

Despite critical raves for both *Red* and for Black Uhuru's live shows, American audiences proved largely indifferent to a seemingly impenetrable foreign culture. The lack of success, coupled with business squabbles, led to the dissolution of what is considered Black Uhuru's definitive lineup. "We'd be one of the strongest reggae bands ever if we could have avoided the jealousies," says Simpson. ❧

24

LOS ANGELES
X
Slash

Producer: *Ray Manzarek*
Released: *April 1980*
Highest chart position: *None*

NO ALBUM HAS SUCCEEDED BETTER as a snapshot of a city and its punk subculture than X's debut album, boldly titled *Los Angeles*. From the William Burroughs cut-and-paste sex and violence of "Johnny Hit and Run Paulene" to the Beverly Hills sleaze of "Sex and Dying in High Society," X depicts a morbid, kicks-oriented demimonde going up in flames. "All those songs are from actual incidents," says singer Exene. "They're not just made up."

In all essential respects, X's *Los Angeles* was not that different from the city Jim Morrison celebrated and damned in his work with the Doors. In fact, the Doors' keyboardist, Ray Manzarek, became X's producer. "I thought Exene was the next step after Patti Smith," Manzarek told writer Richard Cromelin. "She takes it further than any woman has ever taken it."

After being passed over by many major labels, the group signed with the small Slash Records and cut *Los Angeles* – with Manzarek producing and playing keyboards – for the low-budget sum of $10,000. The musical core of the group was punkabilly guitarist Billy Zoom, powerhouse drummer D.J. Bonebrake and bassist John Doe. Exene's untrained but arresting voice entwined with Doe's pitch-perfect vocals in unique harmonies that veered from normal intervals to dissonance. "We ended up with a reckless, offbeat kind of sound that was pretty at the same time, which is an unusual combination," says Exene. Before long, the same labels that had rejected the band were involved in a bidding war to sign them, and X was on its way to leaving a mark on the Eighties with a string of albums.

Doe and Exene, who had independently migrated to Los Angeles from the East Coast, wrote so compulsively about their adopted city because they had never seen anything quite like Los Angeles or its punk-misfit culture. "Any time you're twenty years old and in a big city for the first time, you're going to be writing up a storm," says Exene. "The thing I found incredible about Los Angeles was the flagrant inequality. You'd be on the Sunset Strip with people dangerously close to attacking you for money while all these Rolls-Royces were going by. You just feel like everybody's insane there. No one really has any values. They just make up a little story to act out, and that's their life." ❧

25

TUNNEL OF LOVE
Bruce Springsteen
Columbia

Producers: *Bruce Springsteen Jon Landau and Chuck Plotkin*
Released: *August 1987*
Highest chart position: *1*

BRUCE SPRINGSTEEN WASN'T A ROMANTIC young kid anymore. He couldn't write songs about hitting the road with his girl, because as he got into his late thirties, that wasn't the kind of thing that appealed to a married millionaire. So on the heels of his blockbuster *Born in the U.S.A.* and the ensuing live box set that summarized the past ten years, Bruce Springsteen made a low-

key, intimate record about adult relationships. "It's easy for two people to lose each other in this tunnel of love," he sings ominously on the title track.

"When I wrote the record," he told ROLLING STONE after its release, "I wanted to write a different type of romantic song, one that took in the different types of emotional experiences of any real relationship. Really letting another person into your life, that's a frightening thing. That's something that's filled with shadows and doubts, and also wonderful things and beautiful things."

Tunnel of Love deals mostly with shadows and doubts. Ten years after *Darkness on the Edge of Town*, Springsteen was singing in the voice of a man who, in the words of the remarkable "Brilliant Disguise," is "lost in the darkness of our love." At the center of the album is "Walk Like a Man," an open account of his wedding day. Surrounding the hope at the heart of that song are songs whose characters can barely keep their hopes alive: "Tunnel of Love," "One Step Up," the searing, hard-luck rocker "Spare Parts" and the fearful late-night reverie "Valentine's Day."

"I suppose it doesn't have the physical 'reach out and grab you by the throat and thrash you around' of, say, *Born in the U.S.A.*," said Springsteen. "It was more meticulously arranged than anything I've done since *Born to Run*. I was into just getting the grooves."

It also came quickly. Unlike the modus operandi for most of his albums, Springsteen wrote only three or four extra songs, and he recorded the album swiftly, cutting most of the tracks in a small studio at his home in New Jersey. It was a quintessentially low-tech studio: Springsteen's Corvette had to be moved out of the way to do some piano overdubs.

Springsteen's first series of demos included nine of the album's twelve songs. "Brilliant Disguise" and "One Step Up" came later, and "Tunnel of Love" was written when Springsteen decided that it would make a good album title.

Most of the tracks were recorded, instrument by instrument, by Springsteen himself; though he later brought in E Street Band members and the odd outsider to add parts or replace drum machines, other musicians were used sparingly, and the entire band never played together. As a result, *Tunnel of Love* has an intimacy per-

fectly suited to the tales being told by a rock star determined to return to a more human scale in his music.

"The way you counteract the size [of stardom] is by becoming more intimate in your work," he said. "And I suppose that's why after I did *Born in the U.S.A.*, I made a record that was really addressed to my core audience, my longtime fans." ☙

BACK IN BLACK
AC/DC
Atlantic

Producer: *Robert John "Mutt" Lange*
Released: *July 1980*
Highest chart position: *4*

WHEN AC/DC ENTERED THE STUDIO IN 1980 to cut *Back in Black*, its sixth American album, the band was nervous and uncertain about the future. Its longtime lead singer, the notorious Bon Scott, had choked to death in February following a drinking binge. The band members found a replacement in Brian Johnson, but they were still "a bit

jittery," according to guitarist Angus Young. The gravel-voiced Johnson immediately clicked with the rest of AC/DC, and *Back in Black* surpassed all expectations, becoming one of the milestone hard-rock albums of the decade.

From the ominous tolling that opened "Hells Bells" to a closing blast of defiance titled "Rock and Roll Ain't Noise Pollution," the ten songs on *Back in Black* rock out with brute force and raunchy humor. "Let Me Put My Love Into You" and "You Shook Me All Night Long" may seem blasphemous to some, but AC/DC's lascivious frankness was part of a tradition passed down to rock from the blues. Besides, the down-under rockers were only writing about what they'd seen and heard on the road. Angus Young, who formed AC/DC in 1973 at the age of fourteen with older brother Malcolm, got an eyeful at an early age. "We were in Australia, which at that time was still a bit outback," says Young. "It was just a way of life, a way of talking, and that's how we communicated with the audience." Angus picked up pointers about the guitar from his brother George, a member of the Easybeats (of "Friday on My Mind" fame), and got the novel idea of performing in a schoolboy's uniform – blazer, short pants and beanie – from his

sister Margaret, who for years had watched him run in the house, grab his guitar and run out the door without bothering to change clothes. "At first I thought, 'This is stupid,' " Young recalls. "But the moment I put it on, it

was like Clark Kent and Superman. The suit gave me confidence: I could be another person and go, 'Well, it's not *me*,' you know?"

Back in Black came at a time when the band, through constant touring, had carved out a sizable audience. An instant success, the album entered the British charts at Number One and climbed to Number Four in the States – an exceptional showing for a heavy-metal album – and ultimately went on to sell 5 million copies worldwide. The members of AC/DC saluted Scott, their fallen comrade, by using *black* in the title and on the album jacket. "We didn't want to put *in memory of*, because Bon wasn't that sort of person," says Young. His loss inspired AC/DC to rock harder than ever – and to party somewhat more temperately. "I think we calmed down a bit," says Young. "But if there's a party, we can still put on a good show." ❧

21 APPETITE FOR DESTRUCTION
Guns n' Roses
Geffen

Producer: *Mike Clink*
Released: *July 1987*
Highest chart position: *1*

"WHO WOULD HAVE EVER THOUGHT that the least likely to succeed would make it onto the Top 100 of the decade?" says Slash, the lead guitarist of the Los Angeles renegades Guns n' Roses. He has every right to savor the irony: Only a few short years before their debut album was recorded, the members of the band were living in well-documented druggy squalor, just one among many hard-rock bands looking to get a break on the competitive Los Angeles club scene.

But Guns n' Roses – a shotgun marriage between two bands, L.A. Guns and Hollywood Rose – have an edgy dynamism that sets them apart from the pack. Led by a tattooed former delinquent named Axl Rose, Guns n' Roses play not so much pure metal as unalloyed hard rock that listeners who cut their teeth on the Rolling Stones and the New York Dolls can appreciate.

The dozen songs on *Appetite for Destruction* embrace contradictions in the band members' still-evolving characters, some aspects of which are none too pleasant to contemplate – e.g., the mounting drug habit described with indifference in the matter-of-fact "Mr. Brownstone." The opening number, "Welcome to the Jungle," describes the god-awful Pandora's box of street life for urban runaways with a cynical, scarifying leer. Numbers such as "It's So Easy," with its offhand decadence and driving beat, are real crowd arousers, releasing the venomous rage toward society – and toward themselves – that Guns n' Roses feel they have in common with their fans. During a performance in England at an outdoor heavy-metal festival, two audience members were stomped to death in a mass slam dance while Guns n' Roses played "It's So Easy."

"The sincerity of the band shows," Slash told ROLLING STONE in 1988. "That's why the crowds are so fuckin' violent. Not that I condone crowd violence and riots, but it's part of the energy that we put out."

The other side of Guns n' Roses is the unabashed sentimentality of "Sweet Child o' Mine," a ballad about a girlfriend sung by Rose with undisguised emotion. *Appetite for Destruction* is five talented misfits' way of coming to terms with the world – shouting, screaming and playing as hard as is humanly possible. The fact that it found a sizable and rabidly enthusiastic audience so quickly – the album has gone platinum eight times

over – says that there are many, many kids out there who feel disenfranchised, disillusioned and confused about life in the Eighties. Guns n' Roses are singing their song. ❧

28

CONTROL
Janet Jackson
A&M

Producers: *Jimmy Jam, Terry Lewis, Janet Jackson and Monte Moir*
Released: *January 1986*
Highest chart position: *1*

"THIS IS A STORY ABOUT CONTROL: MY *control*." So begins Janet Jackson's musical diary about her coming of age.

Growing up in America's first family of pop music, Janet began writing and playing at the age of nine. But *Control* was her declaration of independence from a family in which a musical career was expected and all business and career decisions were made by an autocratic father. "The *Control* project represents the first time that I chose to use my ideas on one of my albums," Jackson says.

Jimmy Jam, who coproduced the album with his partner, Terry Lewis, says that the singer desperately desired to make an album that would demonstrate she was capable of standing on her own.

"She wanted to separate from her past two albums, where she had been a singer with no say-so," says Jam. "She was also getting out of a bad marriage and about to start living on her own, away from her family. Being a singer and entertainer was something she had been thrust into before she actually knew that was what she *wanted* to be."

Working with Jam and Lewis at their Minneapolis studio, Flyte Tyme, provided an excellent environment for such a break. "She came to Minneapolis with just her friend Melanie," says Jam. "There were no bodyguards, no limos. She drove herself around in my Blazer. She didn't have people doing things for her."

Only one of the album's songs, "He Doesn't Know I'm Alive," penned by Flyte Tyme staff writer Spencer Bernard, was in hand when the sessions began. "We worked on the album for two months," says Jam. "But we spent the first week just talking and getting to know each other." Those conversations – in which Jackson talked about her desire to be independent – provided the material for the songs on *Control*, most of which were co-written by Jam, Lewis and Jackson. Actual recording time for the album, which would eventually sell more than 5 million copies in the U.S., was just three weeks.

Jam says he had no idea that *Control* would find such a broad audience. "We knew it would be a successful black album," he says. "We tried to make the hardest, funkiest black album – almost a male singer's album. The edginess that's evident in the music on *Control* is her; that's our interpretation of Janet."

Although Michael Jackson's *Thriller* had sold 40 million copies worldwide just a few years earlier, Jam says they felt little pressure about working in the shadow of Michael's accomplishment. "Our joke was that we were out to make it so that Janet was no longer Michael's little sister," says Jam, "but rather that Michael was Janet's big brother."

Control succeeded in establishing Janet Jackson as an artist in her own right. Jam also views the album as a late-Eighties watershed in popular music. "It opened radio to funk," he says, "and now that has spread into rap. Before *Control* it wasn't acceptable to have hard-edged black music on pop radio. Now it's the norm." ❧

29

DOUBLE FANTASY
John Lennon and Yoko Ono
Capitol

Producers: *John Lennon Yoko Ono and Jack Douglas*
Released: *November 1980*
Highest chart position: *1*

IT IS, OF COURSE, IMPOSSIBLE TO separate the album from what happened immediately after it was released. In late November 1980, John Lennon made his musical return after five years of self-imposed retirement with *Double Fantasy*, a full-fledged collaboration with his wife, Yoko Ono; on December 8th of that year, he was murdered on his way home from a recording studio. Rather than being his comeback, *Double Fantasy* became Lennon's sweet, gentle farewell.

But it would have been a rock & roll event regardless. After a self-indulgent, eighteen-month "lost weekend," a separation from Ono and a few disappointing albums, Lennon had retreated into a life of domesticity in late 1975, devoting himself to being a househusband and a father to his son Sean.

In the spring of 1980, Lennon and Sean sailed to Bermuda for a brief vacation; there Lennon became intrigued by New Wave musicians like the Pretenders, Lene Lovich and Madness. And when he heard the B-52's song "Rock Lobster," he was spurred to action. "It sounds just like Ono's music," he told ROLLING STONE, "so I said to meself, 'It's time to get out the old axe and wake the wife up!'"

Lennon would write a song, call Ono in New York and sing it to her; she would answer with a new tune she had written. They wrote more than two dozen songs in three weeks, then recorded two albums' worth of material at the Hit Factory, in New York City. He went into the studio, Lennon later said, "not to prove anything but just to enjoy it."

The result was structured as a dialogue – one song by Lennon, then one by Ono – that dealt with their trials, their separation and, above all, their love. Despite the tensions brought to the surface in songs like Lennon's "I'm Losing You" and Ono's "I'm Moving On," most of the album deals with the contentment Lennon enjoyed once he had left the music business behind. "No longer riding on the merry-go-round," he sings in the marvelous, contemplative "Watching the Wheels," "I just had to let it go."

Initial critical reaction was not unanimously favorable. Some early reviewers attacked *Double Fantasy* for its cozy domesticity, and several other

prominent pans were written but withdrawn from publication after Lennon's death. But in the end the album proved to be durable not just as – in the words of ROLLING STONE contributor Stephen Holden – "an exemplary portrait of a perfect heterosexual union" but as a lovely picture of the happiness two artists had found in each other. "I cannot be a punk in Hamburg and Liverpool anymore," said Lennon three days before his murder. "I'm older now. I see the world through different eyes. I still believe in love, peace and understanding, as Elvis Costello said, and what's so funny about love, peace and understanding?" ❧

30 HOW WILL THE WOLF SURVIVE?
Los Lobos
Slash / Warner Bros.

LOS LOBOS

how will the wolf survive?

Producers: *T-Bone Burnett and Steve Berlin*
Released: *October 1984*
Highest chart position: *47*

"THE 'WOLF' RECORD WAS VERY PIVOTAL for us," says Louie Perez, one of the four East L.A. high-school buddies who started Los Lobos in 1973. "We decided to take a responsible look at what we represented as Mexican Americans. Was this band going to be a fun, sock-hop party band or actually show they're of reasonable intelligence and concern?"

The answer turned out to be both. On *How Will the Wolf Survive?*, Los Lobos – Perez on drums, guitar and requinto; David Hidalgo on vocals, accordion and guitar; Cesar Rosas on vocals, guitar and mandolin; and Conrad Lozano on bass and guitarron – played with crisp exuberance. They adroitly mixed blues rave-ups like "Don't Worry Baby" with traditional numbers such as "Serenata Nortena" and personal songs by Perez and Hidalgo about the band's quest to retain its Mexican American heritage while working within a glossy pop-star industry.

Los Lobos (Spanish for "the wolves") had quit various local cover bands, bought traditional Mexican instruments at pawnshops and learned the *norteño* music of their forefathers. They eventually incorporated electric instruments and in 1983 with the Blasters' saxophonist, Steve Berlin (who soon joined the band), recorded an EP called *...And a Time to Dance*. It sold only 50,000 copies but won many critics' awards.

Hidalgo and Perez worked on songs for their first full-length album at the home of Perez's brother-in-law. "We'd sit down with a guitar, a tape recorder and a jar of Tasters Choice, and we were coffee achievers all afternoon," says Perez. One result of these sessions was "A Matter of Time," a touching ballad about a Mexican crossing the border, looking for a better world.

They entered the studio early in the summer of 1984 with T-Bone Burnett, who had coproduced the previous EP with Berlin. When the record was nearly finished, Los Lobos hit on its title track. Perez found inspiration in an old issue of *National Geographic* with a story entitled "Where Can the Wolf Survive?" "It was like our group, our story: What is this beast, this animal that the record companies can't figure out?" says Perez. "Will we be given the opportunity to make it or not?"

On the way home from the studio late one night, Perez and Hidalgo began writing the song, which was recorded with Weather Report's Alex Acuna on percussion. In it, Hidalgo sings, "It's the truth that they all look for/Something they must keep alive/Will the wolf survive?"

The grace note that pulled the album together was an instrumental of Hidalgo's performed on Mexican instruments. Perez named it "Lil' King of Everything," he

says, because "it sounded to me like this hobo who wakes up in the morning, sees the world and feels good about himself. He doesn't own anything, but he's the 'Lil' King of Everything.'" The seventy-nine-second song was spliced into the intro of "How Will the Wolf Survive?" – linking Los Lobos's Mexican roots, their rocking present and their stellar future. ❧

31

AVALON
Roxy Music
Warner Bros.

Producers: *Rhett Davies*
and Roxy Music
Released: *June 1982*
Highest chart position: *53*

THE SOFT, DREAMLIKE SCOPE OF ROXY MU-sic's 1982 release *Avalon* was a far cry from the band's abrasive Seventies albums. But with its haunting melodies and hypnotic rhythms, *Avalon* was the logical extension of a style that Roxy Music had begun dabbling in on their preceding album.

"*Avalon* was the culmination of a method that was started halfway through *Flesh*

and Blood," says former Roxy guitarist Phil Manzanera. The band holed up in Manzanera's newly built Gallery Studio, in Surrey, southwest of London, and began to experiment.

"We constructed a lot of tracks out of improvisations," Manzanera says. "In the studio, you can head off into very strange territories by artificial means. By accident, you can plug something into the wrong place and something amazing happens that you could never have dreamed of. The combination of writing in the studio while using the studio as an instrument had evolved halfway through *Flesh and Blood* and on into *Avalon*. It was this soundscape to which Bryan would then write his sort of dreamy lyrics."

The album contained some of vocalist Bryan Ferry's strongest songwriting to date. "I think Bryan decided he wanted a more adult type of lyric," says Manzanera. "We were making music that was a bit rockier, but then we decided – in light of the way Bryan was thinking lyrically – that we should tone it down, so it ended up having a more constant sort of mood. And although that mood wasn't very up and rocky, it was positive."

Ferry's lyrics expressed a marked openness and vulnerability. "It was just before he got married," says Manzanera. "It was a period when he was searching."

The title track commences with a subtle reggae lilt. "When we were recording

the third or fourth album in London," says Manzanera, "we'd often be working in the same studio as Bob Marley, who'd be downstairs doing all of those famous albums. It just had to rub off somewhere." Singer Yanick Etienne, recruited while the band was overdubbing in New York, added soaring vocals to "Avalon."

"More Than This," the opening song, was initially poppier, according to Manzanera. "Halfway through, Bryan rebelled, and it was all scrapped and simplified incredibly," he says. "I must say, I was concerned that we weren't going to have a hit single from that album. And obviously, wanting to make it in America, we needed to have a single to break us. But in the context of the whole album, Bryan obviously had a broader view in the back of his mind. By the time it was done, it fit in much better with everything."

The atmosphere in the studio was charged, as was usually the case at Roxy's

sessions. "Roxy Music was a series of complex personalities, and inevitably there would be ups and downs," says Manzanera. "Any sort of creative force that's worth its while has to exist in a sort of state of conflict. So it's absolutely amazing that we managed to do seven or eight albums."

His fondest memory of recording *Avalon*? "The day it was finished." ❧

32

UH-HUH
John Cougar Mellencamp
Riva / Polygram

Producers: *John Cougar Mellencamp and Don Gehman*
Released: *September 1984*
Highest chart position: *9*

BY 1983, JOHN COUGAR WAS A SMASH with the public – his multiplatinum *American Fool*, the biggest-selling album of 1982, saw to that – but was still scorned by critics. With *Uh-huh*, he turned a corner, winning over even hardened skeptics who thought he would never escape the shadow of the heartland-rocker triumvirate of Seger, Springsteen and Petty. Not only did he surmount his influences, he upped the ante with insightful and incisive songs about life in working-class America such as "Pink Houses" and "Authority Song." And, in a move consistent with the no-nonsense, back-to-the-roots flavor of *Uh-huh*, he even reclaimed his real surname, becoming John Cougar Mellencamp. Suddenly other artists were being compared to *him*.

A rough-hewn gem, *Uh-huh* was "written, arranged and recorded during a sixteen-day blowout at the Shack," according to the liner notes. The Shack, in fact, wasn't a studio at all but a half-finished house standing in the middle of Indiana farmland. It belonged to a friend who couldn't afford to finish building it, so Mellencamp agreed to do so for him – provided Mellencamp could rehearse and record there for a year.

Before recording *Uh-huh*, Mellencamp produced a Mitch Ryder record, *Never Kick a Sleeping Dog*, at the Shack. Working with a Sixties icon like Ryder helped gear Mellencamp and company for a leaner, more aggressive sound when it came time to do their own record.

Ironically, one of *Uh-huh*'s most memorable songs, "Pink Houses," isn't a rocker at all but a ballad about the contentment to be found in leading a modest life. Inspiration struck Mellencamp on a highway overpass. "I looked down and saw this old man, early in the morning, sitting on the porch of his pink shack wth a cat in his arms," he says. "He waved, and I waved back. That's how the song started."

"The first time we ever played it is the way it stayed," says guitarist Larry Crane. "We said, 'Well, we got that one,' and we didn't bother it after that." ◈

33

ZEN ARCADE
Hüsker Dü
SST

Producers: *Spot and Hüsker Dü*
Released: *July 1984*
Highest chart position: *None*

WITH THIS LANDMARK 1984 ALBUM, THE
Minneapolis trio Hüsker Dü picked
hardcore punk up out of its monotonous
rut and drop-kicked it into the future.
Structurally, *Zen Arcade* is defiantly anti-
punk – a double album with an operatic
narrative and unorthodox segments of
acoustic folk, backward tape effects and
psychedelicized guitar à la the Beatles'
White Album. Yet in challenging the

rigid hardcore aesthetic of "loud 'n' fast
rules," Hüsker Dü created a brave new
music that was true to punk's raging energy while articulating the anger, confusion and fear of a generation that had
outgrown "Blitzkrieg Bop." The result
was *Tommy* by way of CBGB.

"We started out as a punk
band," said Bob Mould, the
band's singer and guitarist, in
1985. "We had a real garage
mentality about everything.
We'd get pumped up, and a
song that was generally mid-
tempo would come on full
throttle. We didn't have a lot of
control over that sort of thing."
Indeed, the Hüskers' 1981 debut album, *Land Speed Record*,
set the thrash-rock standard.
But, as Mould pointed out,
"hardcore is basically music for
young people. We were growing up, and
[*Zen Arcade*] showed a lot of that."

Hüsker Dü's coming of age took place
during the summer of 1983 in an empty
church in St. Paul, where the band created
Zen Arcade's twenty-three songs. "There
was so much change," drummer Grant
Hart said in 1986. "We were constantly
jamming. We'd pick a chord, any chord,
and then go for it. 'Reoccurring Dreams'
[*Zen*'s frenzied instrumental climax] would
go on for an hour."

The album, primarily written by Mould
and Hart, was recorded the following October in a mere eighty-five hours. All but
two songs were first takes, and the mixing
was done during forty straight hours of

work. Total cost: $4000. Yet the depth
and detail of the story belied the economy
with which it had been committed to tape.

According to Mould, *Zen Arcade* is
about a young computer hack from a broken home who dreams about killing himself after his girlfriend dies of a drug over-
dose. Instead, he lands in a mental hospital
where he meets the head of a computer
company who hires him to design video
games. "Then he wakes up and goes to
school," Mould said. "The only thing we
never agreed on was the name of the video
game. We thought it was Search."

While the story is fictional, Mould allowed that the songs contain elements of
autobiography. "Some of us are from
broken homes, some of us have had
friends die," he said. "I don't think that's
anything new."

But the power and imagination with
which Hüsker Dü married fact and fantasy
on *Zen Arcade*, and the album's subtext of
striving and hope, helped elevate punk to a
higher, more expressive plane. "It's an ad-
mission of humanity," said Mould, who has
gone solo since the band's breakup in early
1988. "You can't just scream and holler all
your life. You have to step back a minute,
look at yourself and say, 'Yeah, I am
fucked.' And try to change it." ◊

34

TATTOO YOU
The Rolling Stones
The Rolling Stones / Atlantic

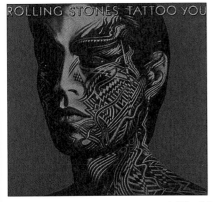

Producers: *Mick Jagger and Keith Richards*
Released: *August 1981*
Highest chart position: *1*

" 'TATTOO YOU' WASN'T REALLY AN Eighties album," says Mick Jagger, and in a sense he's right. The decision to launch a Rolling Stones tour in 1981 left the band with little time to write new songs and prompted what Keith Richards calls "a frantic search through the can" to come up with material for an album – a search that produced some ironic results.

"The album came out and everybody said, 'It's the freshest-sounding Stones album in years,' " says Richards, laughing. "We all had a good chuckle."

"Oh, that made me *really* laugh," Jagger says in agreement. "But now all can be revealed. I was actually rather scared at times. I thought, 'They're bound to notice. The critics can't *not* notice that this is from here and that's from there.' "

As it turns out, the band reached back nearly a decade for material. The ballads "Waiting on a Friend" and "Tops" were begun in Jamaica in 1972 during work on *Goats Head Soup*. "Worried About You" and "Slave" dated back to some 1975 rehearsals in Holland for *Black and Blue*. Early versions of "Start Me Up" were worked up during the *Some Girls* sessions in 1978. Finally, "Neighbors," "Heaven," "No Use in Crying," "Little T&A," "Hang Fire" and "Black Limousine" were initially recorded during the 1979 sessions for *Emotional Rescue*.

Of course, the varied origins of the songs on *Tattoo You* do not detract from the album's power and thematic richness. As Richards points out, having a stockpile of worthwhile material is "one of the advantages of being around for a while." Both Jagger and Richards estimate that forty or more takes exist of "Start Me Up" – one of the Stones' best singles – all but one of which treat the song as a reggae number. "We'd obviously gotten pissed off with reggae," says Richards with a laugh. "We just hit it that one time – rock & roll – and there it was lying there, like a little gem."

In addition to unearthing a single that would burn *Tattoo You* into the memory of their fans, the Stones pushed the boundaries of their music by bringing in jazz saxophonist Sonny Rollins to play on three tracks off the album. "Instead of having all these rock players, I thought we'd go a bit more off the wall and ask him to do some solos," says Jagger. "You can't beat using the best people." In addition, Jagger credits Bob Clearmountain, who mixed the record, for the cohesiveness of *Tattoo You*. "He did a great job of making it all a rather more homogeneous sound," Jagger says. "It sounds crisp, like it was

recorded only yesterday."

For Jagger, *Tattoo You* provided a valuable lesson in the uses of the past. "It just shows what you can do," he says. "Just bring the tracks out, and start doing vocals and the odd guitar bit and saxophones, and then, hey, you've got an album. And it does actually hold up quite well." ❧

35 KILL 'EM ALL
Metallica
Megaforce / Elektra

Producers: *Paul Curcio, Metallica and Mark Whitaker*
Released: *May 1983*
Highest chart position: *120*

WITH ITS 1983 DEBUT, 'KILL 'EM ALL,' Metallica rose up from the heavy-metal underground to establish a vital new subgenre, known as speed metal or thrash metal. As pioneered by Metallica, it was a hybrid of punk and metal, distinguished by lightning speed, manic rhythm changes and a thoughtful if outraged approach to lyrics about suicide, religion, war and nuclear holocaust.

At a time when most young metal bands still slavishly imitated aging or absent gods like Ozzy Osbourne and Led Zeppelin, such songs as "Whiplash," "Hit the Lights" and "Seek and Destroy" were refreshing and revelatory. The no-sellout attitude of the band – singer-guitarist James Hetfield, lead guitarist Kirk Hammett, bassist Cliff Burton and drummer Lars Ulrich – inspired metal fans seeking new thrills and heroes.

Kill 'Em All, originally released on Megaforce and later reissued on Elektra, was the product of what the band calls "riff tapes." Riffs that emerged during practice or jam sessions were committed to tape. Then Ulrich and Hetfield constructed songs from the best riffs. "You start at the top and figure what vibe the song has," Ulrich told ROLLING STONE last year. "The general tempo, where you want to take it all. Get an opening. And at one point soon after the opening, you enter into the Mighty Main Riff."

Hetfield's lyrics, by comparison, were the result of "drinking and thinking, seeing what's going on around me." He tackled weighty subjects like spiritual isolation ("No Remorse") and bloody apocalypse ("The Four Horsemen"). The title of the album certainly captures the adversarial tone of the record, although not as graphically as the name the band originally proposed: *Metal up Your Ass*.

At the time, Metallica had temporarily relocated from California to New York City, where, according to Hammett, the band members lived on bologna sandwiches and Schlitz Malt Liquor while rehearsing and recording. "When we started out, it seemed like all the odds were against us," says Hammett. "The sound we had was so different, other people didn't know what to do with us." When Megaforce told the band that distributors wouldn't go for an album called *Metal up Your Ass*, Hammett says, "we were so pissed off that one day Cliff just went, 'Aw, why don't we just kill 'em all?' And we went, 'Yeah, that's it!' " ❧

36 RAPTURE
Anita Baker
Elektra

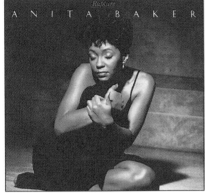

Producers: *Michael J. Powell*
Marti Sharron and Gary Skardina
Released: *March 1986*
Highest chart position: *11*

ALTHOUGH ANITA BAKER'S 'RAPTURE'
exudes an aura of dimmed lights and
romantic introspection, the album was, in
fact, a product of hard times and difficult
decisions. Baker had previously cut a funk
record with a band called Chapter 8 and a
solo album called *The Songstress*, which was
released on the Beverly Glen label in 1983.
When she moved to Elektra, a legal battle

ensued that threatened to block the
release of *Rapture*.

"You don't see any of that turmoil in
the music," says Baker. "It's as if it were an
outlet for more beautiful things." Baker
moved to Elektra because she was looking
for creative freedom. "I knew
what I wanted to sing, and I
knew what kind of production I
wanted, which was a minimalist
approach," Baker says.
"The dilemma was choosing
a producer."

Baker turned to Michael J.
Powell, the former keyboardist
in Chapter 8, who produced
seven of the eight tracks on
Rapture. Baker herself is
credited as executive producer.
Elektra, meanwhile, let Baker
make the record her way.
"They just gave me my budget
and left me the hell alone," she says,
appreciatively.

Rapture, which was released in 1986, is
an emotionally rich, subtly restrained suite
of songs that merge elements of jazz and
soul, with an emphasis on ballads like
"Sweet Love," "You Bring Me Joy" and
"Been So Long." It is bold in its very
conservatism, and it evokes favorable
comparisons to the work of some of
Baker's idols, such as Sarah Vaughan and
Nancy Wilson. Baker says she was not
concerned about how different
Rapture seemed from much of the music
out at the time. "It didn't cause
me any apprehension," she says with
a laugh, "because I didn't think

anybody was gonna *hear* it!"

Rapture was recorded in a couple of
months, with a good deal of time spent
selecting material and working out
arrangements. Baker still finds the album's
depth of feeling satisfying. "I was very
pleased," she says. "I didn't know I had
that in me. I wanted a smooth product with
energy and heart, but I surprised myself.
There's passion there. I knew I could pop
a note, but the nuances, I think, are what's
important on that album."

Interestingly, despite its torch songs
and paeans to love, *Rapture* ends with the
edgy "Watch Your Step" – one of three
songs Baker wrote or co-wrote. It's a
relatively uptempo R&B number that
warns an inconstant lover, "You better
watch your step/You'll fall and hurt
yourself one day." Baker says: "The last
thing that people hear from you should be
something to stir your emotions, to shake
you up. I don't like to leave people relaxed.

I like to start off relaxing them and then
build up to some sort of crescendo."

Despite her regard for the album,
Baker did not anticipate the multiplatinum
sales *Rapture* earned. "Nobody did," she
says, laughing. "*Nobody*. I've heard people
speak of things like that happening; I've
seen it happen to other people. I'll tell you,
though, it took a hell of a lot of work." ❧

37

MIDNIGHT LOVE
Marvin Gaye
Columbia

Producer: *Marvin Gaye*
Released: *October 1982*
Highest chart position: *7*

IT WAS CONCEIVED AS AN ALBUM ABOUT spiritual and sexual salvation titled *Sexual Healing*, after the song that eventually became one of the biggest hits of Marvin Gaye's career. But the singer's new record company, Columbia, wasn't thrilled with the title, and ultimately neither was Gaye, who worried that such a provocative title would spoil what he hoped would be his comeback.

Gaye dropped the idea but kept the song "Sexual Healing," which he correctly believed from the start would be a hit (it reached Number Three on the *Billboard* pop charts). "They'll be jamming all over the world to this," he told his biographer David Ritz, who collaborated on the song's lyrics.

While *Midnight Love* is not Gaye's masterpiece – that honor belongs solely to *What's Going On* – it is an inspired, mature work from one of the greatest soul singers. Loaded with infectious dance-floor grooves, sophisticated guitar work, third-world rhythms and seductive vocals, *Midnight Love* did indeed prove to be Gaye's comeback. Sadly, it was also the last album he made before he was shot to death by his father in April of 1984.

"Marvin had been living in Europe, and he was influenced by both reggae and the synthesizer work of groups like Kraftwerk," recalls Larkin Arnold, a former CBS Records vice-president who was the executive producer of *Midnight Love*. "He took that and came up with something fresh and unique."

Although *Midnight Love* has an urbane, high-gloss feel, the album was actually conceived and created while Gaye was living in Ostend, a quiet seaside town in Belgium. At first he worked with his brother-in-law, the multi-instrumentalist Gordon Banks;

later the veteran Motown producer Harvey Fuqua (who had discovered Gaye in 1958) was brought in.

Gaye worked sporadically on the album over a nine-month period. "He was stubborn," says Arnold. "He enjoyed the role of the tortured and spurned artist. He stopped working on the album two or three times." Columbia's financial cost for getting Gaye into the studio and keeping him there was high: Arnold puts the cost of recording *Midnight Love* close to $2 million.

Whatever the cost, the album was a hit, selling 2.7 million copies worldwide, more than 2 million of them in the United States. Gaye saw his album – which followed two unsuccessful records for Motown – as a commercial endeavor designed to win back a mass audience.

Although he told the writer Nelson George in 1983 that his "mission" was to "tell the world and the people about the upcoming holocaust and to find all of those of higher consciousness who can be saved," Gaye felt the need to draw everybody's attention with a hit before returning to message music. "This is a chance for the world to recognize Marvin Gaye, so that ultimately I can get my message across," he said. ✎

IMPERIAL BEDROOM
Elvis Costello and the Attractions
Columbia

ELVIS COSTELLO and the ATTRACTIONS

IhMcPdErRoIoAmL

Producer: *Geoff Emerick*
Released: *June 1982*
Highest chart position: *30*

WHEN COLUMBIA RECORDS RELEASED Elvis Costello's *Imperial Bedroom* – the angry young Brit's seventh album in six years – the company took out ads that read, MASTERPIECE? Without question, *Imperial Bedroom* is one of Costello's major artistic statements – and arguably the high point in the career of a prolific musician.

Perhaps reacting to the creative limitations of his preceding album, *Almost Blue* – a disappointing collection of country covers recorded in Nashville – Costello returned to form on *Imperial Bedroom*. It is a far-ranging gem that finds him moving all over the musical map, from the ominous, jazzy "Shabby Doll" to the *Sgt. Pepper*-esque pop of ". . . And in Every Home."

When it comes to *Imperial Bedroom*, Costello is its harshest – and maybe its only – critic. "In retrospect, I feel some of the songs are just not well written enough," he said. "Some of them were attempts to create a little mystery room the listener could go into. And in some cases, the subject matter is maybe too large for the song's own good. 'The Loved Ones' is about the trap of playing to posterity, and it's just too *vague* a subject for a song."

Asked about the Columbia ad, Costello grimaced and said, "There were some ludicrous things claimed on behalf of that record." Some reviewers compared Costello to John Lennon and Paul McCartney (Costello would later collaborate with McCartney), as well as Tin Pan Alley immortals like Cole Porter and George Gershwin.

"It could be momentarily flattering," Costello said of the praise. "But then you realize that some people don't like Cole Porter. It made me very perverse on that tour. I'd be playing amphitheaters in the Midwest, and I'd do eight ballads in a row, only two of which would be mine. In the end, all those comparisons just made things more difficult."

According to Geoff Emerick – the veteran recording engineer for the Beatles and the producer of *Imperial Bedroom* – his approach to recording the album was simple. "We were trying to capture Elvis's spontaneity, because he's a first-take kind of guy," says Emerick. Work at AIR Studios in London proceeded quickly. "Elvis is *very* fast," Emerick says. "When we did the first session, there was an onslaught of something like eighteen songs, which we cut in fast takes. From then on, it was a matter of thinking which ones should we record."

The savage guitar and wordless screaming that link three of the songs on the album's first side – "The Long Honeymoon," "Man Out of Time," "Almost Blue" – was something of an afterthought. "That may have been part of a song we didn't use," says Emerick. "We

just faded it in and out."

Despite the rave reviews, *Imperial Bedroom* yielded no hit singles. Still, it is a favorite of many Costello fans, as well as producer Emerick's. "Elvis is a major songwriter," he says. "He just oozes talent. And we captured Elvis then and there. It was easy – I pulled up the fader, and away we went." ❧

39

ELIMINATOR
ZZ Top
Warner Bros.

Producer: *Bill Ham*
Released: *March 1983*
Highest chart position: *9*

ZZ TOP'S 'ELIMINATOR' WAS THE HANDS-down party album of the decade, pleasing hard-core boogie freaks with its bluesy vamping, tawdry lyrics and chic, trashy videos. You practically had to be in a coma *not* to have found some opportunity to dance to "Legs," "Sharp Dressed Man" and "Gimme All Your Lovin' " in 1983. ZZ Top had enjoyed million-selling albums in the Seventies,

but *Eliminator* outsold all the band's previous releases.

"We still sometimes wonder what exactly did transpire to make those sessions dramatically different," says guitarist Billy Gibbons. "I suppose it might have been a return to playing together as a band in the studio as we did onstage."

Many of the songs were written on tour. "Those dressing-room sessions that so many traveling bands talk about really are invaluable to creating a body of studio work," says Gibbons. The band was determined to keep that dressing-room ambience alive when it went in to record.

Though *Eliminator* was cut at Ardent Recording, in Memphis, Tennessee, a trip to England prior to the sessions influenced the album's sound, with the band taking in synth pop and the intense fashion consciousness of its "new romantic" practitioners. The modern technology inspired the band members to have a go at synths themselves, while the cool threads they had seen on the streets of London inspired them to write "Sharp Dressed Man."

The synthesizers the band began noodling around on at Ardent happened to be primitive analogue models, with lots of wires and dials and no presets. "Curiosity was a real magnet to turning on those things," says Gibbons. "What you got was a bunch of cowpokes on

blues twisting knobs from outer space." But it worked: The synthesizers – layered organically among guitars, bass and drums – contributed to *Eliminator*'s dense, bluesy feel.

Often lyrics were inspired by real-life situations. "Legs," for instance, came about one rainy day on the way to the studio. "There was a young lady dodging the raindrops, and being obliging Southerners, we spun the car around," says Gibbons. "No sooner had we turned around to pick her up – boom! – she'd vanished. We said, 'That girl's got legs, and she *knows* how to use them.' "

Another song, "TV Dinners," was inspired by seeing those very words stenciled on the back of a woman's jumpsuit on the dance floor of a funky nightclub on the east side of Memphis. "I was stunned," says Gibbons, deadpan. "There it is, a gift. Why, other than to inspire us, would she have walked past

sporting TV DINNERS on her jumpsuit?"

As *Eliminator* gathered steam, Gibbons's and bassist Dusty Hill's flowing beards became a symbol of ZZ Top. At one point, the Gillette company offered to pay them to shave off their beards on television. "Our reply was 'Can't do it, simply because underneath 'em is too ugly,' " says Gibbons. ❧

40

WAR
U2
Island

Producers: *Steve Lillywhite and Bill Whelan*
Released: *January 1983*
Highest chart position: *12*

"PUNK HAD DIED," SAYS THE EDGE. "WE couldn't believe it had been swept to the side as if it had never happened, and *War* was designed as a knuckle buster in the face of the new pop."

Indeed, at the time of the album's release in 1983, the anger and anarchy of the late-Seventies punk movement had been replaced by the new romanticism best typified by Duran Duran and Spandau Ballet. Into such tepid waters, U2 dropped its bomb: *War* is a powerful fusion of politics and militant rock & roll, an album that anticipated the political awareness that would come back into vogue as the decade progressed.

With two of U2's best sing-along anthems, "Sunday Bloody Sunday" and "New Year's Day," *War* became something of a *Who's Next* for the Eighties. The album's aggressive sound is highlighted by what bassist Adam Clayton calls "all those helicopter guitars."

Following U2's first two albums, the delicate and ethereal *Boy* and the moodier and disjointed *October*, *War* arrived with the force of a jackhammer ripping into concrete. Rough, hard and metallic, it remains U2's most overt rock album.

"We loved the Clash's attitude early on," the Edge says. "And Richard Hell and the Voidoids, the Pistols. Guitar bands that didn't use blues clichés. I was listening to Tom Verlaine to figure out how to make tough music."

The title itself was arresting, as were its politically inspired songs. "We wanted a record people couldn't just write off," says Clayton. "It was an unsettled time, a year of conflict. Poland was on the news at the time. You looked around and there were conflicts everywhere. We saw a lot of unrest on TV and in the media. We focused on that."

Still, U2 wanted to leave listeners with a feeling of hope. "We wanted love *and* anger," says the Edge. "We

wanted a protest record, but a *positive* protest record."

War was recorded in about six weeks at Windmill Lane Studios, in Dublin, with most of the songs written in the studio. Vocalist Bono improvised lyrics to completed tracks, then refined them. "Bono would sing, and whatever came out would be the starting point," says producer Steve Lillywhite.

Completing the songs was difficult. "It's always hard to finish them," says Clayton. "It takes Bono a long time to commit to a lyric. 'New Year's Day' was a tough one. We had arguments over the vocals. At one stage it wasn't even on the record."

The album's final track, "40," which takes its title and lyrics from the Fortieth Psalm, was literally finished at the last moment, even as the next band scheduled to use the studio cooled its heels. "We were trying to get lyrics down and mix it with people pounding on the door," says Clayton. ❧

41

DOCUMENT
R.E.M.
I.R.S.

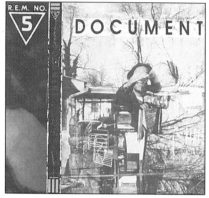

Producers: *Scott Litt and R.E.M.*
Released: *August 1987*
Highest chart position: *10*

R.E.M.'S THORNIEST AND MOST OVERTLY political album, ironically, was the one that brought the band a mass audience, yielding its first bona fide hit single in "The One I Love." After four albums of unique, visionary rock & roll (not counting *Dead Letter Office*, a collection of B sides), the unconventional Georgians left the alternative-music substrata and entered the mainstream, at least saleswise, with *Document* as their passport. As Peter Buck put it at the time, "We're the acceptable edge of the unacceptable stuff."

Recorded in Nashville with producer Scott Litt, R.E.M.'s *Document* is an angry, largely topical look at a world wracked by political and environmental catastrophe. Singing in clear, enunciated syllables, Michael Stipe trains his disapproving lyrics upon despoilers of nature ("Disturbance at the Heron House"), peddlers of right-wing dogma ("Exhuming McCarthy"), warmongers in Latin America ("Welcome to the Occupation") and other abusers of the planet and the public trust. The first side closes with "It's the End of the World As We Know It (and I Feel Fine)," a nervy pop-music news bulletin about an apocalypse in progress. A rapid-fire spew of pop-culture images leads to the main title and its cryptic tag: ". . . And I feel fine."

What was going on? "Michael broached the idea that the stuff he was writing was a little more direct politically," says guitarist Peter Buck, "and the stuff we had been writing was a lot more chaotic, too. It kind of came together."

R.E.M.'s politicization on *Document*, Buck believes, is due to the fact that "your thoughts are obviously different at thirty years old than they are at twenty-three." Even the seeming love song "The One I Love" is far from a fairy-tale view of romance, describing "the one I love" as "a simple prop to occupy my time." "It's definitely not a love song," says Buck. "It's more of a nasty comment about oneself."

Despite its success, "The One I Love" is not one of the band members' favorites. "It's funny that the songs on the radio from us are probably the ones we feel from the heart the least," says Buck. So how did he feel when R.E.M. was proclaimed AMERICA'S BEST ROCK & ROLL BAND on the cover of ROLLING STONE as *Document* was ascending the charts? "Embarrassed, like any sensible person would be," he says with a chuckle. ❧

42 STRONG PERSUADER
The Robert Cray Band
High Tone/Mercury

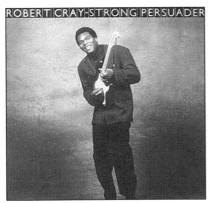

ROBERT CRAY-STRONG PERSUADER

Producers: *Bruce Bromberg and Dennis Walker*
Released: *September 1986*
Highest chart position: *13*

"I THINK THAT MY BAND WAS PART OF A blues-roots movement that included people like the Fabulous Thunderbirds and Stevie Ray Vaughan, who were coming along at that particular time," says bandleader Robert Cray. While Cray's sense of what was happening on the American rock scene in late 1986 is accurate, it modestly downplays the accomplishments of the singer-guitarist and his backing trio.

In February of that year, *Strong Persuader* – Cray's fourth album – hit Number Thirteen on the *Billboard* pop-albums chart, making it the highest-charting blues album since Bobby "Blue" Bland's *Call on Me/That's the Way Love Is*, which reached Number Eleven some twenty-three years earlier. *Strong Persuader*, in effect, introduced a new generation of mainstream rock fans to the language and form of the blues.

An army brat who grew up on bases in West Germany and the Pacific Northwest, Cray was introduced to popular black music at home, but he discovered blues artists on his own as a teenager. "I still have a lot of the same influences today," Cray says. "People like Albert Collins, Buddy Guy, O.V. Wright and Sam Cooke."

In his lyric themes, Cray often veers away from the hard-luck road trod by most bluesmen. But his trebly, razor-sharp guitar playing is straight out of the electric blues tradition, and it provides *Strong Persuader* with a distinctive edge.

Signed to the small HighTone label when work on *Strong Persuader* began, Cray was hoping to hook up with a larger company. "The production on the first records was too low-budget," he says, "and we were looking for a major label because we want to make a better record every time."

Cray and his band eventually cut a deal with PolyGram, but they continued to work with producers Bruce Bromberg and Dennis Walker, who had produced their HighTone albums. As a result, *Strong Persuader* was released with a combined HighTone/Mercury imprint. In addition to coproducing the album, Walker contributed "Right Next Door (Because of Me)," a tale of infidelity played out in a motel room. The song, which became the album's centerpiece, also includes the lyrics from which *Strong Persuader* derived its title.

The song that really drove *Strong Persuader* up the charts, however, was "Smoking Gun," a smoldering tale of jealousy and murder. Although released two months after the album hit the streets – late for a first single – it became a Top Forty hit, and the video became a staple on MTV.

Strong Persuader ultimately went gold, a

feat virtually unheard-of for a blues album. Yet Cray maintains that the album was less a departure from his blues path than a natural evolution. "The recording sessions have been pretty much the same for each of our albums," he says. "I just thought the quality of the music we were making was getting better. It was about the whole band being together." ❧

43

NEBRASKA
Bruce Springsteen
Columbia

Producer: *Bruce Springsteen*
Released: *September 1982*
Highest chart position: *3*

FIRST, HE SAT ON A ROCKING CHAIR IN his New Jersey bedroom, strumming an acoustic guitar and singing into a tape recorder. Then he stuck the cassette (sans case) in his back pocket and carried it around for a couple of weeks. Next, he tried to teach the songs to the E Street Band. Finally, several soul-searching months later, Bruce Springsteen decided that his next album was going to be the cassette tape he'd kept in his pocket.

That tape would become *Nebraska*, an album full of dark, desperate tales from a rock & roll star who'd decided that some stories are best told simply, by a man and his guitar. Commercially, it was a daring move. In 1982, Springsteen was at the point where a strong rock album would have cemented the breakthrough he'd made with *The River*, released in 1980, which yielded his first Top Ten hit, "Hungry Heart." But he was growing increasingly disturbed by the currents in Ronald Reagan's America and was unable to retain his youthful belief that rock & roll could make everything right. "There was a particular moment when I said, 'Oh, my ideas that have sustained me have sort of failed,' " he said later. "I had a particular time when I felt pretty empty and very isolated, and I suppose that's where some of that record came from."

He listened to Hank Williams, Johnny Cash and more obscure folk and country singers. He saw movies like John Huston's *Wise Blood* and Terence Malick's *Badlands*, which sparked his interest in the 1958 murder spree of Charlie Starkweather and Caril Fugate. Back home in New Jersey, he wrote more than a dozen shattering, plain-spoken songs about murder, despair and isolation. On January 3rd, 1982, he sang them, one after another, into a four-track tape recorder.

He planned to teach them to the E Street Band, but somehow the songs that were so haunting in their rough, unaccompanied versions didn't sound right with fuller arrangements. "It became obvious fairly soon that what Bruce wanted on the record was what he already had on the demo," says drummer Max Weinberg. "The band, though we played the hell out of them, tended to obscure the starkness and the vibe he was going for."

Eventually, Springsteen returned to the acoustic demos, deciding to release them as is. *Nebraska* was a grim record for a grim time. It was both a courageous album and an influential one, presaging the frank, narrative songwriting and spare presentation of such late-Eighties folk stylists as Tracy

Chapman and Suzanne Vega. Its ghostly aura even pervaded the work of U2 and John Cougar Mellencamp. But it was, above all, a profoundly personal statement from an artist who was unsettled by all he saw around him — and decided he couldn't look away. ❧

44 OH MERCY
Bob Dylan
Columbia

Producer: *Daniel Lanois*
Released: *September 1989*
Highest chart position: *33*

BOB DYLAN CLOSED OUT THE EIGHTIES with *Oh Mercy*, arguably the strongest album from the singer-songwriter in a decade that saw both his creative ups (*Infidels*) and downs (*Down in the Groove*). Recorded in New Orleans, *Oh Mercy* can be considered a musical trivet consisting of Dylan, producer Daniel Lanois and a solid New Orleans rhythm section.

Lanois, who'd previously worked with U2 and Peter Gabriel, interrupted the recording of his own album, *Acadie*, to work with Dylan. "It's an enlightening experience, watching a great poet embark on a new voyage," says Lanois.

The majority of the album was cut live, with members of the Neville Brothers providing no-nonsense backing for Dylan's raspy, half-spoken vocals. His more cryptic compositions, however, found him accompanied only by Lanois and engineer Malcolm Burn. Although the sessions were shrouded in secrecy, one musician who was there recalls that Dylan was "extremely focused on his writing. He had the lyrics to his songs on a music stand in front of him, and he'd be writing and changing lyrics while people were running around the studio. He does a tune a number of different ways until he hits a groove that works. If things aren't working after a few takes, he goes on to another song."

"Political World" sets the album's lyric theme, boiling with savage musical intensity. *Oh Mercy*'s only other rocker, "Everything Is Broken," is reminiscent of a Slim Harpo blues shuffle, complete with a squeaky harmonica solo. Still capable of making a listener feel squeamish, Dylan chides his audience on "What Was It You Wanted" and "Shooting Star." On the other hand, "What Good Am I" and "Most of the Time" emerge as his most personal compositions in many years.

While it would be unfair to compare *Oh Mercy* to Dylan's landmark Sixties recordings, it sits well alongside his impressive body of work. It is also an encouraging sign that Dylan's creativity will continue to flourish in the coming decade. ❧

45

DAYDREAM NATION
Sonic Youth
Blast First/Enigma

Producers: *Sonic Youth and Nicholas Sansano*
Released: *October 1988*
Highest chart position: *None*

"HOW DO YOU PLAN AN ACCIDENT? That's what we're all about," says Sonic Youth's guitarist Thurston Moore. The trailblazing quartet has made its mark by exploring the rough edges that other bands smooth over, bolstering its experiments in sound with the raw power of a top-flight rock & roll band. *Daydream Nation* refined everything that made Sonic

Youth the most powerful and innovative American guitar band of the Eighties and channeled it into a seventy-one-minute, double-album tour de force. The band's guitarists, Moore and Lee Ranaldo, harnessed an idiosyncratic vocabulary of overtones, harmonics, drones and feedback to create vast sounds and textures unlike anything else in rock.

Daydream Nation is very much of the place where it was created, articulating the chaos and violent energy of the band's New York City. "The structures of *Daydream Nation* were really worked on a lot," says bassist-vocalist Kim Gordon, and sure enough, beneath the music's teeming surface is a Byzantine barrage of spine-tingling riffs and dynamics fueled by drummer Steve Shelley.

Although the largely self-produced *Daydream Nation* was recorded for a paltry $30,000, that was twice as much money as the band had spent on any of its five other albums. According to Gordon, the extra production bucks "gave power to the songs. It's like buying credibility."

"Providence," one of the album's most interesting tracks, is a quiet interlude for phone machine, piano and one abused amplifier. "It was a fan-cooled amplifier," Moore says, "and I had put something on the fan, so the tubes were suffocating and created this panicky rumble coming out of the speakers. So we recorded that and made it into a song." A friend of the

band's, Mike Watt of the group fIRE-HOSE, contributed a phone message from Providence, Rhode Island, scolding Moore for losing some guitar cables and insinuating that his short-term memory was shot. "It's about smoking pot," Moore explains.

Moore says the band originally wanted to call the album *Bookbag* and package it in a plaid schoolbook tote, an idea scrapped only because of its expense. Instead, the band opted for a simple painting of a candle by German artist Gerhard Richter. "We wanted to use something that was outwardly conservative, because people wouldn't expect that," Gordon says.

Both Ranaldo and Moore are veterans of downtown noise maestro Glenn Branca's guitar orchestras. The massed guitars and colossal dissonances of those groups still figure in Sonic Youth's sound, although Moore doesn't quite see it that way: "I mean, he's into the harmonic se-

ries, we're into the TV series." Moore would rather compare his band to the early-Seventies New York grunge rockers in the Godz, whom rock critic Lester Bangs once lovingly described as "the most inept band I've ever heard." "We come straight out of them," Moore says. "If you can find *The Third Testament*, by the Godz, that's a great record." ❧

46

PETER GABRIEL
Peter Gabriel
Geffen

Producer: *Steve Lillywhite*
Released: *July 1980*
Highest chart position: *22*

THE ALBUM'S COVER DEPICTS THE FACE of Peter Gabriel disintegrating ghoulishly, but it is the social and psychological issues explored on Gabriel's third solo album that make it such a chilling work. The album's opening track, "Intruder," is about a thief and potential rapist; "Family Snapshot" is about an assassin; "I Don't Remember" is about an amnesiac; and

"No Self Control," Gabriel's favorite track on the album, is a desperate tale of anxiety, alienation and latent violence. Small wonder that Atlantic Records president Ahmet Ertegun asked if Gabriel had spent any time in a mental hospital after hearing "Lead a Normal Life," an eerie sketch of life in an asylum.

Less understandable, however, was Atlantic's decision not to release Gabriel's third album. (Each of his first four solo albums is titled *Peter Gabriel*.) "I think they were looking for, perhaps, 'Solsbury Hill' or 'Modern Love' – something that they thought had more pop appeal," Gabriel says. "I still have a lot of respect for Atlantic, based on their history. But at the time it was a major blow to my self-confidence. I definitely felt it was my best work, so I was waiting for an enthusiastic reaction, not to be dropped from the label."

Mercury eventually released the album in the summer of 1980; it was well received and enjoyed prominence on alternative radio, largely on the strength of "Games Without Frontiers," Gabriel's jaunty examination of the similarities between childhood play and adult warfare.

Peter Gabriel's jagged rhythms and off-kilter melodies provide a gripping sonic complement to the album's edgy themes. "There were some definite ambitions with arrangements, going for

sounds that hadn't really been used before," Gabriel says. "I think for me as a writer, it's the album on which I discovered a style."

He also discovered "good working partners," among them guitarist Robert Fripp, drummers Jerry Marotta and Phil Collins (Gabriel's old band mate from Genesis), singers Paul Weller of the Jam and Kate Bush, producer Steve Lillywhite and engineer Hugh Padgham. "There was a lot of open minds, a lot of support for exploration," Gabriel says.

Peter Gabriel is perhaps best known today for its closing number, "Biko" – a tribute to freedom fighter Steven Biko, who was murdered in prison by the South African authorities. "I was quite uncertain about getting engaged in a political song," Gabriel admits, "because I'd never directly taken on an issue in that way. I just tried some ideas, and I felt the spine tingling. That to me is the musician's rubber stamp – the spine tingle." After all the troubling themes the album confronts, "Biko" ends *Peter Gabriel* on a stirring note by exalting the indomitable human desire for freedom. That process is part of what Gabriel says is "a familiar theme for me: looking into the darkness and seeing if there's a possibility for triumph." ❧

47

TINA TURNER
Private Dancer
MCA

Producers: *Rupert Hine*
Terry Britten, Martyn Ware
Greg Walsh and Carter
Released: *May 1984*
Highest chart position: *3*

PERHAPS THE MOST SPECTACULAR comeback album of the Eighties, *Private Dancer* reestablished Tina Turner as one of rock's premier artists. But perhaps the most remarkable thing about the album is that it was made at all.

Turner was playing Las Vegas and selling few records when, in 1982, Martyn Ware and Greg Walsh of the English synth-pop group Heaven 17 recruited her for an album of high-tech covers of their favorite songs sung by their favorite singers. Turner's version of "Ball of Confusion" became a British hit and won her a recording contract. Back with Ware and Walsh, her reworking of Al Green's "Let's Stay Together" proved a hit, and Capitol wanted an album fast.

Terry Britten, an Australian songwriter, co-wrote the feisty "Show Some Respect," produced a stark electro-version of Ann Peebles's "I Can't Stand the Rain" and co-wrote the reggae-tinged "What's Love Got to Do With It."

Rupert Hine, known for his work with the Fixx, produced the Holly Knight-penned "Better Be Good to Me." Turner related her life story and her belief in reincarnation to Hine's girlfriend and songwriting partner, Jeanette Obstoj, who then wrote the album's opening track, "I Might Have Been Queen." Lyrics like "I look up to my past/A spirit running free/I look down and I'm there in history/I'm a soul survivor" must have rung true, for as Turner's manager, Roger Davies, says, "she just loved it – I think she almost cried when she read the lyrics."

Mark Knopfler donated "Private Dancer," and British singer Paul Brady wrote the album's hardest rocker, "Steel Claw." Jeff Beck, backed by Dire Straits (minus Knopfler, who had other commitments), contributed electrifying leads to both tracks.

Recording with Britten in London by day and at Hine's country studio by night, Turner cut nine tracks in three weeks. When it was all done, "What's Love Got to Do With It" hit Number One, and "Better Be Good to Me" and "Private Dancer" went Top Ten. *Private Dancer* went platinum several times over, and Tina Turner's rightful place in pop's pantheon was reaffirmed. ✍

48

SKYLARKING
XTC
Geffen

Producer: *Todd Rundgren*
Released: *March 1987*
Highest chart position: *70*

"THIS IS GOING TO SOUND POMPOUS AND arty," says XTC's Andy Partridge, "but the whole album is a cycle of something: a day or a year, with the seasons, or a life. It's a cycle of starting, aging, dying and starting again." He is referring to *Skylarking*, the British trio's superb eighth album.

Recorded largely at Todd Rundgren's studio in Woodstock, New York, *Skylarking*'s fourteen songs abound in elemental imagery and music that is pastoral, understated and carefully arranged. The album is a celebration of nature and particularly of summertime.

"The atmosphere of the album is one of a playfully sexual hot summer," says Partridge. "On a hot day, a lot of life is going to be made somewhere, and it's probably gonna be outdoors on grass. It's just about summer and being out in the open and discovering sex in a stumbly, teenage way."

The concept of the album as a song cycle is underscored by musical interludes and incidental sounds between tracks. The songs are related by key, tempo and subject matter. Oddly enough, the thematic framework was not the band's idea but producer Rundgren's. Guitarist Partridge and bass player Colin Moulding, XTC's principal writers, had worked up thirty-five songs, which they sent Rundgren in advance of their arrival in America. He selected fourteen of them, decided on a lineup and instructed the band to be ready to cut them in that order.

"He tended to go for the gentler songs, for songs of a certain atmosphere," says Partridge. "We'd sit down and talk about where the emotion was headed: the emotion, the atmosphere, the heat, the geographic place, the time of day – this journey you're supposed to go through on the whole record."

Partridge's iconoclastic "Dear God" was left off the album at his insistence. Relegated to the B side of a twelve-inch single, "Dear God" generated such an overwhelming response when played on radio that it became XTC's unlikely first hit in America – and was added to later pressings of *Skylarking*. "I thought I'd failed to précis the largest subject in man's mind, which is man's belief of what the truth is," Partridge says. "How the hell do you condense that into four minutes?"

Skylarking, as it turned out, was the album that broke XTC to a larger audience in America – and it couldn't have come at a more opportune time. "We were at our lowest ebb, moralewise, because we weren't selling any records and it wasn't the LP that Virgin and Geffen wanted made," Partridge says. "They wanted a slick, hard, American rock album: The quote was 'Can you make it somewhere between ZZ Top and the Police?' "

Though subdued and sublime, *Skylarking* was not an easy album to make. The

band members argued with Rundgren and one other; Moulding actually quit at one point, and Partridge repeatedly threatened to fly back to England. Though he didn't like the album initially, Partridge's opinion of *Skylarking* – and of Rundgren – has softened. "I now see with the benefit of hindsight that it's a fine album and he did some sterling work," says Partridge. ❧

49 CRAZY RHYTHMS
The Feelies
Stiff

Producers: *Bill Million*
Glenn Mercer and
Mark Abel
Released: *August 1980*
Highest chart position: *None*

" 'CRAZY RHYTHMS' IS APTLY TITLED," says Bill Million of the Feelies. "There are a lot of weird things going on. We didn't practice much, so we were kind of disjointed when we made the album." Today, *Crazy Rhythms* is a landmark of jangly, guitar-driven avant-pop, and its shimmering sound can still be heard in bands like R.E.M. But it almost wasn't released at all.

The Feelies formed in 1976 in their small hometown of Haledon, New Jersey, as a lark. Tripping on acid one day, Million passed guitarist Glenn Mercer's garage and was impressed to hear the band playing the Stooges' "I Wanna Be Your Dog." The like-minded guitarists formed a band that eventually included bassist Keith Clayton and drummer Anton Fier.

"The sound we were after was a reaction against the punk scene," says Mercer. "Being a little older, we felt it had all been done before. We wanted the guitars to be cleaner, and we started experimenting with a lot of percussion."

Afer recording a four-song demo, the Feelies signed with England's Stiff Records, the only label that would let the fledgling band produce itself. They entered New York's cavernous Vanguard studios late in the summer of 1979 only to find that they couldn't get a guitar sound they liked. "It was very old, things were breaking down," says Mercer. "We tried closets, bathrooms, hallways." Finally, engineer Mark Abel suggested bypassing the amp and plugging the guitars directly into the mixer. "It's a basic rule of recording to never, ever record direct," says Mercer. "It's a very dry, clean sound, and most people think it lacks dynamics. But we found it was closer to your ear, more up front."

The music is jittery, thumping and volatile, complementing titles like "The Boy With Perpetual

Nervousness" and "Loveless Love." There are long silences, repeated notes, wavering tones, pickups flipped on and off. Any gaps are filled with strange, found percussion instruments, including cans, shoe boxes and coat racks.

Their record label, however, "hated it," according to Mercer. "They brought us into a meeting, put Lene Lovich's latest song on the turntable and said, 'You guys gotta come up with something like *this*.' " The album received little promotion, Fier was soon wooed away by the Lounge Lizards, and the band broke up for several years. Today, *Crazy Rhythms* is available only as a German import. "People have talked about remixing and re-releasing it," says Mercer, "but you don't want to mess around with it. It's got a life of its own." ❧

50 MADONNA
Madonna
Sire

Producers: *Reggie Lucas*
John "Jellybean" Benitez
and Mark Kamins
Released: *August 1983*
Highest chart position: *8*

FIVE YEARS AFTER ARRIVING IN NEW York City from her hometown of Pontiac, Michigan, Madonna Louise Ciccone had little to show for a lot of work. By 1982, she had managed to get only a few gigs singing with drummer Stephen Bray's band, the Breakfast Club, at clubs like CBGB and Max's

Kansas City, and the future looked far from bright.

"I had just gotten kicked out of my apartment," Madonna says, "so the band let me live in their rehearsal space at the Music Building, on Eighth Avenue. Stephen had keys to all the rehearsal rooms, so when I decided to make my own demos, we'd go into other people's studios at night and use their four-track machines."

Armed with a tape, Madonna began making the rounds of New York's dance clubs. "I had heard that a lot of A&R people hung out at the clubs," she says, "and I thought trying to go see them at their offices would be a waste of time." It proved a good strategy: Through Mark Kamins, the DJ at Danceteria, the tape found its way to Sire Records, and Madonna was signed by label president Seymour Stein. "Seymour was in the hospital at the time," she says. "I got signed while he was lying in bed in his boxer shorts."

The contract with Sire guaranteed just one single, but it had options for recording albums as well. With Kamins producing, Madonna cut the moody disco track "Everybody" as her debut single. But when Sire picked up its option to record an album, she decided to try a different producer. "I wanted someone who'd worked with a lot of female singers," she says.

Reggie Lucas, the Grammy-winning songwriter who had produced Stephanie Mills and Roberta Flack, was selected. After recording the album's second single, the Lucas-penned "Physical Attraction," he and Madonna cut the rest of the album, with the exception of "Holiday," which was produced by Jellybean Benitez.

"Things were very informal and casual," Lucas says of the sessions. "It was my first pop project, and she was just a new artist. I had no idea it would be the biggest thing since sliced bread."

Indeed, initial response to *Madonna* gave no indication of the mania to follow. It took a year and a half for the album to go gold. But its assured style and sound, as well as Madonna's savvy approach to videos, helped the singer make the leap from dance diva to pop phenom, and it pointed the direction for a host of female vocalists from

Janet Jackson to Debbie Gibson.

"It influenced a lot of people," says Madonna, who cites Chrissie Hynde and Debbie Harry as her own musical heroes. "I think it stands up well. It just took a long time for people to pay attention to me – and I thank God they did!" ❧

51

RUN-D.M.C.
Run-D.M.C.
Profile

Producers: *Russell Simmons and Larry Smith*
Released: *March 1984*
Highest chart position: *53*

THE PIONEERING RAP-METAL FUSION OF the song "Rock Box" and the powerful 1984 debut album it came from, *Run-D.M.C.*, catapulted nineteen-year-old rappers Run (Joseph Simmons), D.M.C. (Darryl McDaniels) and their DJ, Jam Master Jay (Jason Mizell) – to the top of the rap heap and beyond. "Rock Box" proved that rap, like rock, is a malleable art form, capable of absorbing other influences, continually reinventing itself in the process.

Run and D.M.C. wielded rhymes like rockers wield guitars; the hugely influential "Rock Box" made the comparison explicit by souping up an inspired brag session with an innovation: blistering heavy-metal guitar from ace sessionman Eddie Martinez.

Although Run thought it was a bad idea at first, the marriage of metal and rap was inevitable, as rappers had already been using rhythm tracks from songs such as Billy Squier's "Big Beat" and Aerosmith's "Walk This Way." "Rock Box" kicked down musical barriers: It was the first video by a rap artist on MTV, thereby attracting a large white audience.

The rap-metal fusion remained influential. In the summer of 1986, Run-D.M.C.'s remake of "Walk This Way" went Top Five. The Beastie Boys rode rap metal to platinum heaven with hits like "Fight for Your Right to Party," and Tone-Lōc's "Wild Thing," with its Van Halen guitar hook, went double platinum early this year.

Run-D.M.C. includes several other rap classics as well. The group's first two singles, "It's Like That" and "Hard Times," paint bleak pictures of unemployment, inflation and war but go on to promote school, work and church as a way out. But the positive message wasn't simply a public service. "I was trying to get a record that was positive," Run says, "because I knew that the radio didn't want to play anything negative."

On tracks like "Sucker M.C.'s," Run and D.M.C. rapped over little more than an infectious drum-machine beat spiced up with synthesized hand-claps, capturing on vinyl what rappers had been doing in New York City parks for years. Although radio initially bridled at the minimal approach, the record's hip street sound eventually proved irresistible, giving creedence to Run's assessment of the album: "It's good to be raw."

Run's brother, Russell Simmons, who went on to become rap's foremost impresario as co-owner of Def Jam Records, helped arrange the vocals and coproduced the album with Larry Smith, a veteran R&B musician who programmed the drum machines and supplied the odd organ swoosh. Jam Master Jay scratched in

percussion effects while the two rappers took a novel tag-team approach, uncannily finishing each other's lines, phrases and even words.

Besides some heavy breathing, Smith made a unique contribution to "Wake Up." "If you really listen to the record," Smith says, "you'll hear somebody peeing in the toilet and flushing it. That was me!" ☙

MAKING MOVIES
Dire Straits
Warner Bros.

DIRE STRAITS   MAKING MOVIES

Producers: *Jimmy Iovine and Mark Knopfler*
Released: *October 1980*
Highest chart position: *19*

"I LOVE DOING THIRD ALBUMS," SAYS Jimmy Iovine, who coproduced Dire Straits' *Making Movies* with the band's lead singer, guitarist and songwriter, Mark Knopfler. "A group makes its first album, and then the record company rushes them into the studio to make their second album. After that, they go, 'Whoa, wait a second.' They get a little more confident.

They step back and say, 'Okay, *now* we're gonna do it.'"

Iovine's description is an apt summary of the road Dire Straits traveled to get to *Making Movies*, which followed the band's distinctive 1978 debut, *Dire Straits*, and its disappointing second album, *Communiqué*. The description also captures the nature of Knopfler's ambitions for the record. "I think he wanted to take Dire Straits to that next step, especially in terms of the songs, and to have the album really make sense all together," Iovine says. "It's a really cohesive album. He stunned me, as far as his songwriting talents."

Knopfler contacted Iovine because he liked Iovine's work on "Because the Night," the Patti Smith single that she'd co-written with Bruce Springsteen. Iovine, who had also worked on *Born to Run* and *Darkness on the Edge of Town*, was instrumental in calling E Street Band keyboardist Roy Bittan into the sessions for *Making Movies*. Without him, the album's cinematic power and evocative landscapes might have been impossible to achieve.

The melodicism and romantic intensity of Bittan's playing alternately underscore and serve as a foil for Knopfler's guitar – and help elevate such tracks as "Romeo and Juliet," "Tunnel of Love" and "Expresso Love" to poetic heights. Bittan's role became especially

important because Knopfler's brother David, the band's rhythm guitarist, left Dire Straits during the first week of recording. Guitarist Sid McGiniss was brought in to assist Mark, bassist John Illsley and drummer Pick Withers, but Bittan was the first keyboardist the band had ever fully worked into its lineup.

"Mark was real excited, because it was the first time he expanded Dire Straits in a way that has been consistent since then," Bittan says. "It was a seminal album for them in that respect."

Bittan describes the sessions for *Making Movies* as "work sessions where we went in and really took time to capture the emotion and paint the picture. The subtleties of emotion that he was trying to capture was something real special – it reminded me of Bruce, you know?"

Making Movies was recorded in six weeks, but, Iovine says, "it basically happened on the first six days of the sessions. The right people were in the room together. It really was making a record in the pure sense of the term. The whole thing sounds like one song. But you know what that is? That's the writing, the guy who wrote it. He *wrote* the album like that; he wanted to make the album like that." ❧

53 BRING THE FAMILY
John Hiatt
A&M

Producer: *John Chelew*
Released: *May 1987*
Highest chart position: *107*

JOHN HIATT MADE HIS BEST ALBUM, THE skillful *Bring the Family*, in record time – four days in February 1987.

On it, Hiatt was accompanied by a small, simpatico ensemble of all-star musicians: guitarist Ry Cooder, bassist Nick Lowe and drummer Jim Keltner. The sessions were preceded by no rehearsals or preproduction. Lowe, in fact, went straight from the airport to the studio, arriving just in time to cut "Memphis in the Meantime," a song he had never heard before. The spontaneity of it all, Hiatt believes, was largely responsible for the understated, forthright collection of songs that resulted. "I just don't think it would've come out the same if we'd spent more time on it," he says. "The beauty of the project was that none of us was given the time to think with the old left side of the brain."

Producer John Chelew imposed a four-day limit on the sessions; his motivation had less to do with economics or scheduling than a desire to capture the performances with an unstudied, first-take freshness. Hiatt himself likens it to a jazz session, where a band runs a tune down a few times, cuts it and moves on. "I imagined it might be something similar to that, in terms of the intensity and the fun," Hiatt says. "It was kind of scary, too, but very exciting."

There were seat-of-the-pants decisions made at every turn. When the band couldn't settle on an arrangement for the moving, confessional "Have a Little Faith in Me," Hiatt banged it out alone at the piano during a break, and it wound up on the album in that form. Lowe's breathless arrival the first day gave "Memphis in the Meantime" its odd, loopy rhythms.

Hiatt is especially fond of *Bring the Family*'s love songs. Having beat his alcohol and drug problems in 1984, Hiatt was a clearheaded, happily married and much less vituperative songwriter. " 'Learning How to Love You,' for instance, is a song I had never been able to say quite so directly," Hiatt says. "I'm a coward, basically, when it comes to love, and that was the first time I really felt willing to come out and be a little vulnerable."

The emotional openness and spiritual resurgence carried through the whole album – which, amazingly enough, was made at a time when Hiatt didn't even have a record deal in America. "The normal sort of pressures of making a record, real or imagined, just weren't there," says Hiatt. "I'm not so sure a major label would have even let it happen, frankly, although they all seemed to want it after we made it."

To the contrary, *Bring the Family* is one of the most sublime and deeply felt albums of the Eighties. "I think the effect this group of musicians had on each other is that we all wanted to do our best," Hiatt says. "I'm not trying to feign humility, but the way I look at the album today, I really see it as a true collaboration. It's a very inspirational bunch. I would like to go on record to say I sure hope it happens again." ❧

54 SPEAKING IN TONGUES
Talking Heads
Sire

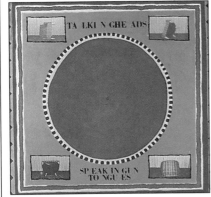

Producers: *Talking Heads*
Released: *June 1983*
Highest chart position: *15*

" 'SPEAKING IN TONGUES' WAS A lighter record," says Talking Heads singer David Byrne, referring to the band's 1983 release. "I guess we wanted to show that we weren't totally one-sided. We were in danger of being categorized as a kind of quirky, gloomy bunch of weirdos."

The band's playful side indeed shines through on the album's nine songs, which include such tracks as the wobbly "Making Flippy Floppy," the animated "Girlfriend Is Better" and the cheery "This Must Be the Place (Naive Melody)." For all its lightheartedness, however, the album still managed to fuse the band's disparate musical interests, most notably the Afro-funk that Byrne had led the band to explore on its preceding album, *Remain in Light*, and the dance-oriented sounds that drummer Chris Frantz and bassist Tina Weymouth had pursued with the Tom Tom Club. And years of touring had given the Heads a sense of how to craft songs that would appeal to their audience.

"By playing live, you figure out what it is that makes people jump up and down and what it is that makes them sit in their chair," says Frantz. "When it came time to do *Speaking in Tongues*, we knew we were going out on the road. It's not like everything is premeditated, but we had this feeling that it's not just about art. It's also about entertainment. When we went out on tour after that, it was the first time that the kids would go nuts for the songs off the current album. In the past they'd go for the old ones, like 'Psycho Killer' and 'Take Me to the River.' "

The band wrote the tracks at the Blank Tapes recording studio in New York. "The writing was done by four people sitting down in a studio and just rolling the tape," says Frantz. "We'd record these long, extended grooves and then bring in people like Alex Weir to add a little bit of additional guitar and various other people, like keyboardist Wally Badarou."

Byrne sang nonsense lyrics, which he later refined. "I sang all the words in gibberish first," he says, "and then made words to fit later. I'd done that a little bit before, but it was the first time I'd done it for a whole record."

"Some of the gibberish actually made sense," says Weymouth. "Certain phrases like 'I've got rockets in my pockets,' on 'Moon Rocks,' actually remained on the record from the first improvisational takes. We didn't want to lose them, because they were so free and they fit right in."

The chorus in the opening song, "Burning Down the House," was inspired by a Parliament-Funkadelic show. "I heard these kids in the audience screaming, 'Burn down the house,' " says

Frantz, "and I thought, 'Wow, that sounds like a song.'

"I guess it was a good title, because I heard it on classic rock radio twice today," Frantz says now. "They won't play our new stuff, but they'll play the old stuff. Hey, it *was* a classic title. But what we really wanted to do was rock the house." ❧

55 CENTERFIELD
John Fogerty
Warner Bros.

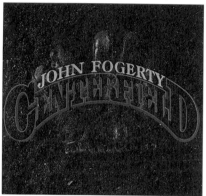

Producer: *John Fogerty*
Released: *January 1985*
Highest chart position: *1*

JOHN FOGERTY BEGAN RECORDING *Centerfield*, the album that revived his long-dormant career, right after he attended the major-league-baseball All-Star Game at San Francisco's Candlestick Park in the summer of 1984. Fogerty's seats were, he notes, in center field. "I was very aware of the connotation of center field – the comeback, spotlight angle of it," says Fogerty. "It all seemed very Zen-like and cosmic to me at the time."

Fogerty's hopes were, of course, rewarded. *Centerfield* went on to become his first Number One album since his departure from Creedence Clearwater Revival, and two of its singles, "Old Man Down the Road" and "Rock and Roll Girls," went Top Twenty. The album found Fogerty at the top of his form, and it contains songs that rival his best work from CCR's glory days.

Centerfield shows Fogerty to be a mature record maker. It is a concept album that can be taken as simply a great collection of songs, a kind of "Whitman's sampler of what John Fogerty is about," as he puts it. But look a little deeper and one finds an intensely autobiographical album: a survivor's tale that celebrates the durability of rock & roll and the power inherent in remaining true to one's own beliefs.

While some of the songs on *Centerfield*, like "Rock and Roll Girls" and "Big Train (From Memphis)," evoke lost innocence, others cynically portray Fogerty's experiences in the music business. The title of "Vanz Kant Danz," which was originally named "Zanz Kant Danz," refers to Saul Zaentz, the head of Fogerty's former record label, and "Searchlight" chronicles the emotional toll the CCR years had taken on Fogerty. But the story Fogerty tells on *Centerfield* has a happy ending. The title track, of course, is the centerpiece of the album, a song about getting another chance at the big time, and "I Can't Help Myself" expresses the excitement John Fogerty felt at once again being a player on the rock scene.

Fogerty had been trying to write songs for an album for years, but he says they just didn't come together. Toward the end of 1983 he finally regained his muse. "Stuff just suddenly started to click," he says. "So much so that I began to think, 'I'm gonna be able to make a record pretty soon.' " He came up with about twelve songs but narrowed the song list down to the nine that appear on the album.

The actual recording of *Centerfield* took two months at the Plant, in Sausalito, California, and cost just $35,000. Because Fogerty worked from detailed demos and notes, recording was straightforward and painless. "*Centerfield*, probably more than any record that will ever be made, is a result of one guy's homemade production," says Fogerty. "Here's a case where the guy who wrote the songs literally put all the little sprockets on the drums. Each thing was actually hand-done by me." ◆

56

CLOSER
Joy Division
Warner Bros. / Qwest

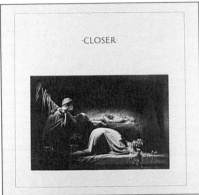

Producer: *Martin Hannett*
Released: *July 1980*
Highest chart position: *None*

"IT'S A HEAVY ALBUM," SAYS BERNARD Sumner, who played guitar and keyboards with Joy Division and still can't listen to *Closer.* "It was a voyage into the dark side of yourself."

"Decades," the masterpiece that closes the record, seems to tell of that voyage: "We knocked on the doors of hell's darker chambers/Pushed to the limit, we let ourselves in/Watched from the wings as the scenes were replaying/We saw ourselves now as we never have seen."

The eerie soundscapes and fatalistic lyrics on *Closer* (re-released on Warner/Qwest Bros.) take listeners down into the abyss and challenge them to crawl back out. Metal machine rhythms and twisted, tortured guitars echo Ian Curtis's anguished vocals, while synthesizers add a feeling of steely, high-tech alienation and a bleak sense of space. Peter Hook's bass often carries the melody, an innovation much copied since – there's not a doom rocker around who doesn't owe something to Joy Division, but they're just gray imitations of a deep, dark band.

"Mother I tried/Please believe me/I'm doing the best that I can/I'm ashamed of the things I've been put through/I'm ashamed of the person I am," Curtis sang on "Isolation." As if to prove he really meant it, Curtis took his life soon after the album was recorded, hours before the band was to embark on its first American tour (the band changed its name and carried on as New Order).

Joy Division's powerful first album, *Unknown Pleasures,* had topped the British independent charts in 1979, yet the members of the band weren't fully satisfied with the sound of it. "We wanted it to be more powerful," says Sumner. Less than a year later they recorded *Closer.* Curtis acted as musical director; as Sumner says,

"The madder the music sounded, the more pleased he would be with it."

The members of the band would sleep all day and work through the night, undisturbed, until dawn, when twittering birds would sometimes find their way onto the studio tapes. Sumner says that while they were recording a room sound, they picked up a phantom whistling the tune of "Decades" – odd, since the building was otherwise deserted. Figuring it was a bad omen, they left it off the record.

Ironically, Curtis dropped hints about his fate, yet no one could decipher them. He once told Sumner, "I feel like I'm caught in a whirlpool and I'm being dragged down and there's nothing I can do about it." "But he wouldn't explain what he meant," says Sumner. "I think he wanted someone to help him, but he didn't want to ask." ❧

EMPTY GLASS
Pete Townshend
Atco

Producer: *Chris Thomas*
Released: *April 1980*
Highest chart position: *5*

ON 'EMPTY GLASS,' HIS SECOND SOLO album, Pete Townshend chronicled the personal tumult he was experiencing and initiated an adult style of songwriting that helped reenergize the singer-songwriter tradition in the Eighties.

Eight of the ten songs were written following Who drummer Keith Moon's death late in 1978. In December of 1979, during the band's American tour, eleven fans died in a preconcert crush outside Riverfront Coliseum, in Cincinnati. Meanwhile, the members of the Who were repeatedly dismissed as worn-out ancients by Britain's scornful punks.

Amid the turmoil, Townshend resolved to make a solo album. "In a way, I've got the punk explosion to thank for making that decision," he said in 1987. "It freed me. It allowed me to be myself. It dignified me, in a way, to be cast to one side. I felt uneasy with the way the Who were inevitably on the road to mega-stardom. . . . [It] was the most important thing I've ever done for me — to allow me to have a new beginning, to actually grow."

On *Empty Glass*, Townshend's ambivalent obsession with punk dominates both the lyrics and the music. Produced by Chris Thomas, who'd recently worked with the Pretenders and the Sex Pistols, the album was raw, muscular and focused in a way the Who never would be again.

Although he'd begun a spiral of booze and drugs that would lead to a bout with alcoholism and a temporary split with his wife, Karen, Townshend pledged in "A Little Is Enough" to make the best of their fitful marriage. "I was able to very easily put into words something that had actually happened to me when I was a thirty-four-year-old," he said. "It's very emotional, but it's also very straightforward and clear."

Of course, a literal reading of a songwriter as complex as Townshend can be deceptive, as in "Rough Boys" and "And I Moved" (written for Bette Midler), taken by some as confessions of homosexual lust. Townshend said, "A lot of gays and a lot of bisexuals wrote to me congratulating me on this so-called coming out. I think in both cases the images are very angry, aren't they? In 'Rough Boys,' the line 'Come over here, I want to bite and kiss you' is about 'I can scare you! I can frighten you! I can hurt all you macho individuals simply by coming up and pretending to be gay!' And that's what I really meant in that song, I *think*."

He dismissed "Let My Love Open the Door" as "just a *ditty*," but it charted as high as any Who single ever had, reaching Number Nine. "If I disagree with the fact that [*Empty Glass*] is the best work I've done in a long time, I would be fooling you," Townshend said in 1982. Later, he admitted that the Who seemed much less viable as a result: "I think the only thing that really went wrong was that I realized, as soon as *Empty Glass* was finished, 'Hey, this is it. I'm not able to achieve with the band what I've achieved here.' " ❧

58

THE INDESTRUCTIBLE BEAT OF SOWETO
Various Artists
Shanachie

Compiler: *Trevor Herman*
Released: *June 1986*
Highest chart position: *None*

THE NEXT LOGICAL STEP AFTER YOU'VE gone to Paul Simon's *Graceland*, *The Indestructible Beat of Soweto* is a classic. Out of the bleak and dusty streets of Soweto, South Africa's largest black township, springs music that's joyous and proud – and you can dance to it.

Trevor Herman, an expatriate white South African ("I left for the obvious reasons"), compiled these twelve tracks,

which were recorded in the early Eighties, when a resurgence in township music, known as *mbaqanga*, and consciousness about apartheid propelled the music out of South Africa and won it international acclaim.

Mbaqanga takes its name from a doughy cake sold on township streets – it's very workaday music that deals with everything from drunken husbands to gossips to hard-working miners. "In most parts of Africa," Herman says, "music is more than entertainment – it's part of life. Everything is celebrated in song, in the rhythm of living."

An alloy of several tribal styles as well as jazz and reggae, *mbaqanga* shares a number of similarities with the blues, and not just because it is a music born of oppression. Like modern blues, *mbaqanga* came about when workers flooded into major cities, bringing their local music with them. And like the blues, *mbaqanga* got electrified when it came to the city.

One strand of *mbaqanga* music comes from hymns learned from missionaries, very evident in Ladysmith Black Mambazo's stirring "Nansi Imali" ("Here Is the Money"). There's a lot of reggae in the two tracks by the legendary Mahlathini and the Mahotella Queens, and a country & western sound pervades "Sobabamba," by Udoketela Shange Namajaha.

In the early Sixties, several township styles – jazz, penny-whistle music and *marabi* (honky-tonk music) – coalesced into a dance music that became known as township jive. With a steady beat adorned by droning acoustic guitars, tinkling electrics and rich vocal harmonies that are joyous, gritty and real, *mbaqanga* became party music played in *shebeens* (illegal bars ignored by the government), at workers' parties, on the street and in the recording studio, where groups often united for one-shot recordings. Herman theorizes that the strong beat came from American groups such as the Supremes. "Also, a lot of players were listening to the Beatles," he says. "Not so much the music but the instrumentation."

Since many *mbaqanga* bands are ethnically mixed, their music brings together different black ethnic groups; if South Africa's black majority hasn't

prevailed because it is a house divided, it's not the fault of *mbaqanga*.

In the final analysis, it's inspirational music. "Maybe they're living in hell," Herman says of the *mbaqanga* players, "but when they get down to the music, it's something from themselves, something from the heart, something that gives them strength." ❖

59 COMPUTER GAMES
George Clinton
Capitol

Producer: *George Clinton*
Released: *November 1982*
Highest chart position: *40*

"I WAS HAVING FUN ON THAT ALBUM," George Clinton says of *Computer Games*, which contains blueprints for all the tangents funk and rhythm & blues would take in the Eighties. With a cosmic giggle, Clinton co-opted the new technology – sequencers, samples, remixing, looping and scratching. In addition to reestablishing Clinton early in the new decade, *Computer Games* netted him a comeback hit in "Atomic Dog," a funky ode to man's best friend filled with canine woofing and all sorts of rhythmic trickery that has since been sampled on numerous rap and hip-hop records.

Throughout his four decades in music, Clinton's sales figures have never been a true measure of his influence. In the Seventies he forged a white-rock-black-funk synthesis with the bands Parliament and Funkadelic, much as Sly Stone and Jimi Hendrix had done in the Sixties. Parliament featured horns and was closer to soul, while Funkadelic emphasized guitars and was closer to rock. There were many offshoot projects as well, with Clinton juggling roles as master conceptualist.

In 1981, however, an overworked Clinton put P-Funk on hold and took time off to straighten out personal and legal business. Almost two years later, *Computer Games* announced his return. Clinton worked especially hard on the album to prove that "I still had my brain together," he says. "The minute you get real drunk or wrecked, the first thing you think is 'Oh, Lord, if you let me out of this one, I won't do it no more.' Mine is, I have to be able to cut a record; that's the only thing that will let me know I didn't fuck up. I just had to find that out for myself, and I think I was all right."

In truth, Clinton was often brilliant, giving an Eighties face lift to funk on "Atomic Dog" and looping up a storm on the wild collage of old and new soul songs titled "Loopzilla." "Atomic Dog," which neither Clinton nor the record company viewed as commercial, was a sizable hit. In fact, says Clinton, " 'Atomic Dog' wouldn't get out of the way for any other single off that album." Six years later it remains so popular that Clinton cut another "dog" song – "Why Should I Dog U Out?" – for his latest album, *The Cinderella Theory*. "I figured, 'Let's give 'em some more dog; let's start right off doggin' 'em again,' " Clinton says, laughing. "I thought they had enough of 'Atomic Dog,' but they didn't, so here's some more. With fleas and ticks." ◌

60

THE BLUE MASK
Lou Reed
RCA

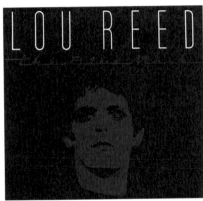

Producers: *Lou Reed and Sean Fullan*
Released: *April 1982*
Highest chart position: *169*

LOU REED'S 1982 ALBUM 'THE BLUE Mask' was "the end of something," as Reed put it in a 1986 ROLLING STONE interview, "the absolute end of everything from the Velvet Underground on. *The Blue Mask* was the final ending and *Legendary Hearts* [the 1983 follow-up] like a coda."

The Blue Mask certainly marked a crossroads in Reed's life and art. In stark contrast to his well-publicized personal and musical indulgences of the Seventies, Reed was now married and enjoying the new-found domestic calm documented in "My House" and "Heavenly Arms," the ballads that bookend the album. At the same time, he had formed a lean, mean quartet combining his own psycho-twang with that of the celebrated New York guitarist Robert Quine and the fluid R&B bass of Fernando Saunders.

The result is a poetically compelling, musically brutish summation of Reed's rites of rock & roll passage. *The Blue Mask* harks back to the twin-guitar violence of the Velvets and Reed's earliest literary conceits ("My House" is dedicated to his mentor at Syracuse University, the poet Delmore Schwartz). At the same time, the album casts a hopeful eye toward the future while effectively closing the book on Reed's extended narrative odyssey through the dark side of human experience – violence ("The Gun"), alcoholism ("Underneath the Bottle") and spiritual isolation (the howling "Waves of Fear"). Reed, who had already written definitive songs about drug addiction and sexual perversion, managed to top himself with the title track, which was packed with graphic images of sexual torture, Oedipal desire and, finally, castration. "I can't even listen to that song," the usually fearless Reed admitted in 1986.

Initially, Reed gave each member of the band a bare-bones demo of the songs for *The Blue Mask*, with Reed singing and strumming an electric guitar. There were no rehearsals as such before the band went into the studio in October 1981. According to Robert Quine, "We'd just go in every day and do at least one, maybe two songs. We'd

start to play and the arrangement would take shape."

To preserve the spontaneity and bare-knuckles sound of the band, each track was recorded live (Reed redid his vocals later) and usually nailed down in two or three takes. "The Blue Mask" itself didn't even take that long. "We did one half-finished take on that one," says Quine, "did another one and that was it. That's a great moment when [Reed] takes that guitar solo at the end. It's every bit as brutal and energized as his stuff with the Velvet Underground." ❧

61

DOC AT THE RADAR STATION
Captain Beefheart and the Magic Band
Virgin / Epic

Producer: *Don Van Vliet*
Released: *September 1980*
Highest chart position: *None*

CAPTAIN BEEFHEART ONCE SAID OF HIS music, "I'm just throwing up – in tie-dye." If so, then *Doc at the Radar Station*, released in 1980, is one of the most colorful, and pivotal, records in his singular catalog. Poised on the cusp of a new decade, Beefheart (a.k.a. Don Van Vliet) poured out his innards in technicolor for *Doc at the Radar Station*, serving up his most colorful and caustic verse in years on a sprawling, dis-

tinctively Beefheartian platter of corrosive avant-rock, jungle-blues squawk, alien-guitar romanticism and willful, yet often playful, atonality. He added a Mellotron to his aural palette, attacking it on "Sue Egypt" and "Ashtray Heart" with the vigor of the Phantom of the Opera. His singing was animated – going from stratospheric screech to subterranean Howlin' Wolf in a heartbeat – and laced with an unmistakable menace.

Doc at the Radar Station is the true heir to Beefheart's epic 1969 masterpiece *Trout Mask Replica*, capturing his remarkable art with power and unprecedented cohesion. Beefheart recognized his own achievement at the time; one *Doc* rocker is proudly titled "Best Batch Yet." And guitarist Moris Tepper, who joined Beefheart's Magic Band in 1975, still believes that the album was the peak of his tenure. "We were able to pull the goo out a lot more clearly than we had earlier," says Tepper.

As always, Beefheart dictated the content of *Doc at the Radar Station* to the Magic Band in obsessive detail, presenting tapes of himself playing the piano, or sometimes just whistling a phrase, and telling the band to interpret it, *exactly*. For "Sue Egypt," Tepper says, there were sections on Beefheart's demo "where he was literally screaming bloody murder into a tape recorder. And then going, 'Here, play this.'"

Guitarist-drummer John "Drumbo" French, who had played on *Trout Mask*

Replica and was already familiar with Beefheart's idiosyncrasies, recalls the rather odd way the band did backing vocals on "Run Paint Run Run." "We didn't have a copy of the lyrics," says French. "We were supposed to be singing these parts, and we didn't know where the heck we were sup-

posed to be singing or what the words were. I think the reason he did that was to get that anger, that kind of screaming out of us. He wanted us to sound really desperate. And it came out real well."

Beefheart's own desperation is evident on the record. "Making Love to a Vampire With a Monkey on My Knee" is a violent lyric climax: "Gnats fucked my ears 'n nostrils/Hit my brain like hones 'n numbed t' nothing. . . . Oh fuck that thing. . . . Fuck that poem!" Yet the album also has moments of remarkable tranquillity, such as Gary Lucas's solo guitar performance on "Flavor Bud Living."

Doc at the Radar Station was, in a sense, Beefheart's last hurrah. After *Ice Cream for Crow*, in 1982, a weary and frustrated Beefheart retired from music to concentrate on painting (he did the cover art for *Doc at the Radar Station*). But when contacted recently, Beefheart said that he still listens to *Doc* a lot. "I'm the music I'm making when I'm painting," he declared. "The paintbrush is my pen now." ❧

62 PYROMANIA
Def Leppard
Mercury

Producer: *Robert John "Mutt" Lange*
Released: *January 1983*
Highest chart position: *2*

THE ALBUM TOOK A YEAR TO RECORD and had to sell 1 million copies just to break even. But Def Leppard's 1983 chart torcher *Pyromania* was worth the time and expense: It sold more than 9 million copies and, with its radio-ready blend of melodic savvy and stadium wallop, defined the mainstream metal sound of the Eighties, for better and worse. For worse because *Pyromania* unleashed a plague of cheap imitators (Poison, Winger and White Lion). For better because the Leppards and their producer, hard-rock auteur Robert John "Mutt" Lange, set precedents in commercially astute songwriting and sheer studio ambition.

"We gave Mutt songwriting credits because this time he actually helped us structure the songs," singer Joe Elliott said in 1985. "He sat down with us as a sixth member of the band."

Lange and the Leppards worked for months on riffs and choruses, trying different combinations and then sewing them up when they made melodic and commercial sense. But the writing wasn't all so academic. "Photograph" was a song with a good chorus, a hot bridge but a flabby verse riff until guitarist Steve Clark started noodling around on his guitar one night while the rest of the band was watching World Cup soccer.

Pyromania was a hard-rock temple built brick by brick. To get a sound that combined metal muscle with studio precision, Lange recorded each member of the band individually. A single guitar riff overdubbed with clean harmonies, funky distortion and screaming feedback might take up to three weeks to record, often one string at a time. When the band members later went to do background vocals, they discovered all of the guitars were slightly out of tune. It was too late to re-record them, so the guitars were put through an electronic harmonizer to cover up the bum notes.

Lange's obsessiveness with the smallest sonic details had a big downside: It was hard to tell, from day to day, whether *any* progress at all was being made on the record. After an all-night session, Lange would often play work tapes for Leppard comanager Peter Mensch, who lived a short drive from Battery Studios. "It got to a point where I'd keep listening to these tapes and I couldn't tell what was there and what was missing," says Mensch.

There were personal complications, too. Founding rhythm guitarist Pete Willis was fired midway through the sessions because of a debilitating alcohol problem; within forty-eight hours, his replacement, Phil Collen of the London glam-rock band Girl, had cut the solo for "Stagefright."

That was nothing compared to the calamity of recording the next LP, *Hysteria*.

That album took *three* years to record; drummer Rick Allen also lost his left arm in an auto accident. Fortunately, it takes more than a little trauma to keep a good Leppard down, as *Pyromania* so ably proved. "There was always that feeling there, that we have to do it right," Rick Savage said a couple of years ago. "Or we don't do it at all." ❧

63

ENTERTAINMENT!
Gang of Four
Warner Bros.

Producers: *Andy Gill, Jon King Rob Warr and Rick Walton*
Released: *May 1980*
Highest chart position: *None*

"THEY OFFER CUT-UP SITUATIONAL accounts of the paradoxes of leisure as oppression, identity as product, home as factory, resident as tourist, sex as politics, history as ruling-class private joke," wrote Greil Marcus in ROLLING STONE of the Gang of Four in 1980. But as the band's drummer, Hugo Burnham, says, "We were also a

great fucking rock & roll band."

The band's propulsive funk riffs ran headlong into jarring stops and starts; singer Jon King's harangues battled Andy Gill's noisy guitar lines; bassist Dave Allen's heavy bottom laid down the law as Burnham pounded out tricky tattoos. The relentless, churning thrust of tracks like "Damaged Goods" and "I Found That Essence Rare" built up unbearable tension, then released it in explosions.

Gang of Four was intent on shattering both musical and lyric conventions – that its driving dissonant music prove danceable was not only necessary, it was also inevitable. "We were using the building blocks of 'rock music,' 'funk music' and 'pop music,' dismantling them to see what was there," Gill says.

And Gang of Four's revolutionary pop rhetoric not only infiltrated the dance floor – it also invaded the corporate world, as the band was one of the few early postpunk outfits to sign to a major label. It was a situation some found hypocritical, but as Burnham says, "If you've got something to say, and you want people to hear it, what's the best thing to do? Make as many people hear it as possible."

The radical musical approach is epitomized by Gill's post-Hendrix feedback on "Anthrax." In his lyrics, King may work in anything, including Godard films, news items, terminology from

video games and TV advertising slogans, to make his points about the effect of Western culture on interpersonal relationships.

The title of the album neatly reflects its own paradox – that of commenting on entertainment *and* being it. The title comes from the song "5:45," in which a man watching the evening news comes to the realization that "guerrilla war struggle is a new entertainment!" It isn't all straight sociopolitics; songs like "Damaged Goods" and "Contract" are about romance, demystified and reduced to a transaction. "Anthrax" contains two separate sets of lyrics sung simultaneously: one song comparing love to a cattle disease, the other a brief essay about why pop music is so fixated on love.

The mood at the studio was hardly convivial – Gill and King helped produce the record, and there was as much jockeying over production credits as good

seats at the mixing console. "It was really vicious, it was hell," Burnham says with a chuckle. "But we got a fucking brilliant record out of it."

Unfortunately, Gang of Four never quite matched *Entertainment!* again and underwent a gradual and messy breakup, leaving behind this postpunk masterpiece as its legacy. ✧

64
VIVID
Living Colour
Epic

Producers: *Ed Stasium and Mick Jagger*
Released: *April 1988*
Highest chart position: *6*

SCREAMING ELECTRIC GUITAR PUNCTU-ates the raucous melodies and street-smart lyrics on *Vivid*, an album that not only marked the auspicious debut of the hard-rocking band Living Colour but was also credited with breaking down racial barriers in pop music. The band proved to be the first black rock group to attract a large mainstream audience since Sly and the Family Stone in the early Seventies, and the album's ascent was accompanied by as much hubbub over the band's ethnic makeup as its compelling style.

"It wasn't like the idea of *Vivid* or Living Colour was generated by some sort of desire to make it in the white world of rock music," says lead guitarist and group founder Vernon Reid. "There was a lot of talk about it. But it's not odd that black people play rock & roll – what's really odd is that people *think* it's odd. It's a shame more people didn't focus on the music itself, because that's what we wanted."

The music itself is an intoxicating brew of hard, grinding rock with splashes of funk, jazz, reggae, rap, punk and even country rhythms. Darting from the hip-hop twang of "Broken Hearts" to the metal assault of "Middle Man," the band refuses to stay stuck in any single groove. *Vivid*'s opening track, "Cult of Personality," is the real kicker, a riff-rock anthem on the harmful effects of idolatry and blind faith that ironically helped turn the band members into pop icons.

The group's seeming overnight success was actually years in the making. Born in England and raised in Brooklyn, Reid earned his musical chops during the early Eighties playing guitar in electric jazz outfits like Defunkt and Ronald Shannon Jackson's Decoding Society. He formed Living Colour as a trio in 1984, going through various configurations for two years before hooking up with singer Corey Glover, drummer William Calhoun and bassist Muzz Skillings. Then came the real stroke of luck: Reid was called in to play on Mick Jagger's solo album, *Primitive Cool*, and the Stone dropped by the New York club CBGB to catch Living Colour's show.

Jagger got so worked up over the set that he took a week off from mixing his own album to produce two demos –

"Glamour Boys" and "Which Way to America?" – for the group. After the Jagger tapes helped Living Colour snag a record deal, the band called in *Primitive Cool* coproducer Ed Stasium to oversee the rest of the album. Jagger came back later to blow harmonica on "Broken Hearts," and Public Enemy's Chuck D. and Flavor Flav delivered a social-commentary rap on "Funny Vibe."

Social issues provided the basis for several numbers, such as the scathing attack on gentrification, "Open Letter (to a Landlord)." But there are also touching love songs ("I Want to Know"), a Talking Heads cover ("Memories Can't Wait") and an offbeat, funky theme song ("What's Your Favorite Color?").

"People say we're a message band," Reid says. "But we're just trying to chronicle a certain thing that was happening with us. That thing about messages – really, the record was about the way we feel." ❧

65

IN MY TRIBE
10,000 Maniacs
Elecktra

Producer: *Peter Asher*
Released: *July 1987*
Highest chart position: *37*

'IN MY TRIBE' — A FEAST OF ACOUSTIC rockers centered around singer Natalie Merchant's alluring vocals and a jangly guitar sound — vaulted 10,000 Maniacs from underground status into the Top Forty. And not a moment too soon, either: The third album from the upstate-New York cult band was literally a make-or-break affair.

"There was a lot of pressure on us," says keyboardist and band cofounder Dennis Drew. "If *Tribe* hadn't been successful, there never would have been another album."

In My Tribe is more than a successful record – it is a poetic, heartfelt message about social concerns such as alcoholism, child abuse and illiteracy.

The Maniacs didn't always have such a passionate sense of purpose. Drew and Steven Gustafson, both college-radio DJs, formed a band called Still Life, which started out covering Joy Division and Gang of Four songs. Merchant joined after wandering into the radio station armed with a pile of LPs she wanted heard on the air. Also recruited were guitarist Rob Buck and John Lombardo, a seasoned composer-guitarist who served as the group's major creative force. Drummer Jerome Augustyniak came on board in 1982, and the group – after changing its name – released an independent EP and album before moving to Elektra Records.

The Maniacs' major-label debut, *The Wishing Chair*, won fine reviews but met with indifference outside alternative-music circles. Lombardo quit under stormy circumstances, and the anxiety proved to be contagious. After rejecting demos for the band's next album, Elektra insisted the group work with producer Peter Asher, best known for his work with Linda Ronstadt and James Taylor.

The shotgun marriage worked out in the end, but it was a shaky trip to the altar. The band felt uncomfortable recording in Los Angeles, Asher's home turf. The Maniacs were also unhappy with many of Asher's additions to their sound, including computerized drums. Asher insists he was merely "cajoling" the band into doing its best work.

Elektra suggested doing a familiar song as the lead single, resulting in a cover of Cat Stevens's "Peace Train." The gambit failed to break the group, and the song was later removed from the album after Stevens – a converted Muslim – called for the death of *Satanic Verses* author Salman Rushdie. The Maniacs ultimately scored with their

sadly lilting second single, "Like the Weather." It took two years for *In My Tribe* to go platinum, but even the band agrees it was better late than never.

"The album gave us a great chance to really coalesce as a band," says Drew. "At that point we had to save our career and make a good record. We fucking buckled up, tightened our belt and did it." ✍

66 FIYO ON THE BAYOU
The Neville Brothers
A&M

NEVILLE BROTHERS

Producer: *Joel Dorn*
Released: *June 1981*
Highest chart position: *166*

KEITH RICHARDS THOUGHT THE
Neville Brothers' *Fiyo on the Bayou* was
the best album of 1981. Most music fans
never had a chance to form an opinion.
"I knew it wasn't going to get played on
the radio," says Cyril Neville. "So I
didn't build up any false hopes. We just
made the best record we could."

With *Fiyo on the Bayou*, the Neville
Brothers — singer Aaron, keyboardist

and singer Art, saxophonist Charles
and percussionist Cyril — set out to
capture their undisciplined sound,
descended from New Orleans Mardi
Gras music, while commercializing it
enough to reach a broad audience.

The tracks on *Fiyo on the
Bayou* can be divided into
two distinct categories: in
the first are dance-floor
burners like "Hey Pocky
Way" and "Sweet Honey
Dripper"; in the second,
showcase ballads for the
band's primo canary, Aaron,
like "Mona Lisa" and
"The Ten Commandments
of Love."

"The first time I saw the
Nevilles was at the Bottom
Line, in New York," says
producer Joel Dorn. "They
completely blew me out of the water."

Dorn pitched a Nevilles deal to
A&M, which initially didn't share the
producer's enthusiasm. "A&M
thought the Nevilles were too ethnic
and too regional," he says.
Concurrently, singer Bette Midler —
whom Dorn had produced and who is
also a Nevilles fan — lobbied A&M on
behalf of the band. The label
eventually gave Dorn the green light.

A self-admitted "sucker" for
Aaron's angelic voice, Dorn
painstakingly surrounded it with lush
orchestration. "When we cut 'Mona
Lisa,' we used the New York
Philharmonic," says Dorn, "and

Aaron sang live in the booth. We
turned out all the lights except for one
spot that was focused on a Nat 'King'
Cole album. He sang the whole song
to that album."

Of course, everyone involved was
convinced he had a hit on his hands. "It
was one of the few times that I've made
a record and was 100 percent satisfied
when we finished," says Dorn. "I felt

Fiyo on the Bayou was the culmination
of my career." But the title of the
album proved confusing. Both Cyril
and keyboardist Art Neville had been
members of the seminal New Orleans
band the Meters, which had released a
1975 album entitled *Fire on the Bayou!*
Inclusion of a new version of the
Meters' signature tune "Hey Pocky
Way" on *Fiyo* further muddied the
bayou. "We wanted those songs to be
heard by more people," says Aaron.

Most radio stations were just as
puzzled by the Nevilles' style, which
didn't fit easily into any programming
format. "We just couldn't get any
airplay," says Dorn. "It was the kind of
record where I wished I could have
gone door-to-door and said, 'Here —
listen to this record!' " ❧

61 TROUBLE IN PARADISE
Randy Newman
Warner Bros.

Producers: *Russ Titelman and Lenny Waronker*
Released: *January 1983*
Highest chart position: *64*

"NOTHING," SAYS RANDY NEWMAN when asked what he had been thinking about when he began work on his eighth album, *Trouble in Paradise*. "I had no cohesive plan in mind."

A cynical tour de force, *Trouble in Paradise* sets several of Newman's nastiest portraits of prejudice, greed, ego and small-mindedness against some of the most striking music of his career. "It came to be about places and situations that could be ideal," says Newman, "but are somehow messed up."

Newman is clearly one of pop music's preeminent songwriters. But with *Trouble in Paradise*, he also mastered the art of great record making. Today it stands as one of the best albums of his career, a fully realized collection of story-songs in which Newman's dark take on the world is fully fleshed out.

Although the best-known song is Newman's love-hate letter to his hometown, "I Love L.A." ("Look at that mountain/Look at those trees/Look at that bum over there, man/He's down on his knees"), *Trouble in Paradise* is full of clever material. "Christmas in Cape Town," with its disturbingly spooky music, is a poignant tale of racism and mean-spiritedness. In "Mikey's," two old-timers complain about what the world is coming to, distressed by the minorities now frequenting their favorite bar. "There's a Party at My House" sounds like a good-time rocker, until the punch line ("Hey Bobby, get the rope"), which hints at kinky escapades.

The centerpiece of the record is "My Life Is Good," which details the self-importance of a Hollywood wheeler-dealer. Asked about the similarities between the song's protagonist and himself, Newman laughs and says, "If I were that big a jerk, I wouldn't admit to it."

The arrangements throughout the album have a cinematic quality (Newman worked on movie scores to *The Natural* and *Ragtime*). "His songs are quite visual," says Lenny Waronker, who coproduced the album with Russ Titelman. "His songs are like little movies. It's like scoring eleven films."

The album includes some impressive cameos: Don Henley, Lindsey Buckingham, Christine McVie, Rickie Lee Jones, Bob Seger, Wendy Waldman, Linda Ronstadt, Jennifer Warnes and Paul Simon all contribute. "His peers have such a high regard for him," says Waronker. "They wanted to be a part of it and help get Randy's stuff out to a lot of people."

How does Newman feel now about *Trouble in Paradise*? "It's a pretty good

batch of songs," he says. "There are things about it I love. Like the first half of 'Miami.' I like the two ballads, 'Real Emotional Girl' and 'Same Girl.' And 'My Life Is Good' – although if I had to do it again, I might not do it the same way. It might be funnier just with piano." ❧

68

THE SPECIALS
The Specials
Chrysalis

Producers: *Elvis Costello and the Specials*
Released: *December 1979*
Highest chart position: *84*

THE SPECIALS FOUND A HAPPY medium between the aggression of punk and the more danceable, upbeat rhythms of ska. Sporting porkpie hats and two-tone suits, the racially mixed seven-member band from Coventry, in Britain, spearheaded a ska renaissance. The Specials' debut album, produced by Elvis Costello, also launched the briefly successful 2-Tone Record label.

The Specials opens with a cover of Robert "Dandy" Thompson's ska anthem "A Message to You Rudy," then dives into more manic numbers, like a gritty version of Rufus Thomas's "Do the Dog" and the band's own "Concrete Jungle."

In his first outing as a producer, Costello captured the spirit of the Specials' frenetic live shows by re-creating a club environment in the studio. "It was a terrific atmosphere," says vocalist Neville Staples of the sessions at London's PW studios. "We just went in and played our show. It was all live in the studio."

In fact, for the song "Nite Club," the band even brought in an audience. "We had roadies, Chrissie Hynde and a few other friends," says Staples. "It was a laugh, because we had a little drink to get the pub atmosphere going."

"We wanted it to be like the first Clash album," said bassist Horace Panter shortly after the album's U.S. release in 1980. "Not necessarily produced, just recorded. Costello was more of an observer, if you like. Suggesting things that we were too involved in to see ourselves."

In addition to its punk-meets-reggae sensibility, *The Specials* is charged with antiracist sentiment: "Just because you're a black boy/Just because you're a white/It doesn't mean you've got to hate him/Doesn't mean you got to fight," sings Terry Hall in the calypso-flavored "Doesn't Make It All Right."

"We were working as a black and white unit," says Staples. "At the time there was a lot of racism happening. So we just thought, 'Well, we went to school with black and white guys. Instead of fighting and calling people names, let's work together.' So we combined black music with punk. We just mixed the two cultures." ❧

69

RADIO
L.L. Cool J
Def Jam / Columbia

Producer: *Rick Rubin*
Released: *November 1985*
Highest chart position: *46*

L.L. COOL J (BORN JAMES TODD SMITH) was seventeen years old when he recorded this early rap masterpiece. Rhymes such as "They hear me, they fear me/My funky poetry/I'm improving the conditions of the rap industry" proved prophetic – *Radio* went platinum, ushering in rap's blockbuster era and heralding the arrival of a superb rapper.

The liner notes say, "Reduced by Rick Rubin," and simplicity was the key to *Radio*. "We were going to bring it down, break it down, reduce it to its most minimal form – like *real* low," says L.L.

But its minimalism wasn't what made *Radio* a rap landmark. Before 1984, most rappers had simply recited continuous rhymes over four minutes of groove. Rubin arranged raps like pop songs, with verses, choruses and bridges. So that L.L.'s rhymes could fit into this new format, Rubin says, "I would say, 'You've got twelve lines, and you've got to do it in eight.' And L.L. would rewrite it so it worked in eight. It was just making rap more like songs."

L.L. Cool J stands for "Ladies Love Cool James"; he became one of rap's first heartthrobs, partly because of his dimpled good looks and macho swagger, but also because *Radio* includes two of the earliest rap ballads, the cuddly "I Want You" and "I Can Give You More."

One of *Radio*'s most powerful tracks is "Rock the Bells." Oddly enough, the track has no bells on it. L.L. was set to record the track using a cowbell break from a song called "Mardi Gras," until Run-D.M.C. used the identical beat on its "Peter Piper." As L.L. puts it, "I got housed." Rubin suggested using a percussion break from the go-go great Trouble Funk instead, and L.L. turned in a ferocious performance; the moment when he yells, "Rock the bells!" and the go-go beat kicks in is one of the most dramatic in rap.

The album's opener, "I Can't Live Without My Radio," became a B-boy anthem. Now that L.L. has reached the advanced age of twenty-two, he says he is still unable to live without his radio. "But now it's in my car – know what I mean?" ✿

TRAVELING WILBURYS VOLUME I
The Traveling Wilburys
Wilbury/Warner Bros.

Producers: *Otis and Nelson Wilbury*
Released: *October 1988*
Highest chart position: *3*

THE TRAVELING WILBURYS' ALBUM WAS one of those happy accidents that was almost waiting to happen. Starting with a throwaway song quickly recorded by George Harrison, Bob Dylan, Tom Petty, Roy Orbison and Jeff Lynne for the B side of a Harrison single, the project soon took on a life of its own. After deciding the track was too good to waste, the veteran

rockers cooked up a full-length album that included some of each member's strongest material in years and became one of the decade's unique musical achievements.

From the catchy folk-pop hooks of the first number, "Handle With Care," to the breezy country-rock finale, "End of the Line," the album's chiefly acoustic tunes all have the sound of instant classics. But the real kicker was the presentation. Rather than releasing the album under their own names, the five musicians hid behind a thin cloak of anonymity, attributing their work to a mythical group and adopting hick personae as part of an elaborate charade.

The five half-brothers of the Wilbury family were hokey but hip, and their individual strengths complemented one another perfectly. There was Orbison (Lefty Wilbury), whose haunting, dynamic vocals are enshrined on the operatic "Not Alone Any More," and who reclaimed his former glory only to pass away shortly after the album became a huge hit. Harrison (Nelson Wilbury) spearheaded the project following his fine solo album, *Cloud Nine*, proving that his comeback was no mere fluke. Dylan (Lucky Wilbury) emerged from a rut of several mediocre albums with his sneering "Congratulations," the jaunty "Dirty World" and a seeming lampoon of Bruce Springsteen, "Tweeter and the Monkey Man." Meanwhile, Petty (Charlie T. Jr.) acted out the role of eager kid

brother, with his fine work on "End of the Line" and the woolly pickup tale "Last Night," presaging his top-selling solo album the following year. Rounding out the quintet was Lynne (Otis Wilbury), the former ELO leader who handled most of the production chores and sang the rockabilly bopper "Rattled."

Lynne remembers how the five musicians usually gathered at Dave Stewart's home studio in Los Angeles and banged out ideas until a complete song resulted from the jamming. "Somebody would say, 'What about this?' and start on a riff," says Lynne. "Then we'd all join in, and it'd turn into something. We'd finish around midnight and just sit for a bit while Roy would tell us fabulous stories about Sun Records or hanging out with Elvis. Then we'd come back the next day to work on another one."

While the Wilburys were intended as a lark, songs like "Heading for the Light,"

"Not Alone Any More" and "Handle With Care" offer idealistic, romantic messages from a fraternity of rock graybeards. "Well, it's alright, riding around in the breeze/Well, it's alright, if you live the life you please," says the opening lyric to "End of the Line." It was a comforting notion indeed, as the uptight, conformist Eighties drew to a close. ❧

11 CROWDED HOUSE
Crowded House
Capitol

Producer: *Mitchell Froom*
Released: *July 1986*
Highest chart position: *12*

IT SOUNDS LIKE IT WAS FUN TO MAKE.
Crowded House's debut album is full of
lighthearted, melodic, enormously catchy
pop songs: "Mean to Me," "World
Where You Live," "Now We're Getting
Somewhere," "Something So Strong" and
its biggest hit, "Don't Dream It's Over."
From start to finish, *Crowded House* is shot
through with the high spirits and sheer
tunefulness of classic pop music.

But it turns out that the album wasn't
so easy to make after all. "It's remarkable
to me that it sounds like a really simple,
easygoing album," says Crowded House
leader Neil Finn, "because there was quite
a large amount of angst involved in making
that record."

Singer, songwriter and guitarist Finn, drummer Paul Hester and bassist Nick Seymour
formed the band after the dissolution of the underappreciated
New Zealand pop group Split
Enz, of which Finn and Hester
were members. They'd been
together for about a year when
they traveled to Los Angeles to
make their debut album for
Capitol Records in 1986 – but
still, says Finn, "we weren't really a band at all. Having come
from a band that had spent ten
years together, it just felt like a collection of
three people at that stage."

They shared a house in the Hollywood
Hills – hence the band's name – and went
to work with producer Mitchell Froom, at
the time best known for his work with the
Boston roots rockers the Del Fuegos.

"They hadn't really decided what they
wanted the record to sound like," says
Froom. "Even the broadest terms – like,
should there be a lot of synthesizers, or
should it be more natural – weren't sorted
out. We just tried different things as we
went along, and it seemed to take on a
character of its own as it went along."

"It was bloody hard work," says Finn,
"partly because it was all so new to me –

new producer, new band, new record company, new town, new everything – that I
was really cautious every step of the way. I
was wary of what Mitchell was suggesting
and second-guessing him, and he wasn't
completely confident with us, either."

A handful of session musicians, including guitarists Tim Pierce and Joe Satriani
(the latter on backing vocals only), were
brought in, and on "Now We're Getting
Somewhere" bassist Jerry Scheff and
drummer Jim Keltner was used.

"At the time that was quite a threatening thing," says Finn. "Paul and Nick felt
quite sheepish about the whole thing. The
next day we recorded 'Don't Dream It's
Over,' and it had a particularly sad groove
to it – I think because Paul and Nick had
faced their own mortality."

The results hardly sounded forced,
though the album seemed to be a flop until
persistent word of mouth and some never-
say-die promotion turned it into a hit eight

months after its release. "It could easily
have not been successful," says Finn. Indeed, the group's follow-up album, *Temple
of Low Men*, failed to garner significant
sales despite strong reviews. "The difference between an album becoming successful and people thinking it's remarkable,"
says Finn, "and being obscure and completely forgotten about is really slight." ❧

12

MARSHALL CRENSHAW
Marshall Crenshaw
Warner Bros.

Producers: *Richard Gottehrer
and Marshall Crenshaw*
Released: *May 1982*
Highest chart position: *50*

"THERE WAS SUCH A FLURRY OF ACTIVITY at that time that I don't actually have too many memories of making the first album," says Marshall Crenshaw of his acclaimed debut effort, which earned him a reputation as a new master of pop-rock songcraft. "All I can remember is my co-producer, Richard Gottehrer, eating a lot of pasta and me pumping Thom Panunzio,

our engineer, for stories about his days working with John Lennon."

After all, only a few years before making his big splash, Crenshaw had been touring the United States as an ersatz John Lennon in various national companies of the successful pseudo-Fab Four musical *Beatlemania*. Tiring of that well-paying gig, Crenshaw decided to work on his own music. By the summer of 1980, Crenshaw – who hails from the Detroit area – was playing his own tunes around New York City as part of a trio, with his brother Robert on drums and Chris Donato on bass.

Crenshaw's homemade demo caught the attention of Alan Betrock of the tiny Shake Records, who put out a twelve-inch single of "Something Gonna Happen" backed with "She Can't Dance." Producer Richard Gottehrer, then much in demand because of his work with the Go-Go's, heard Crenshaw's demo and had rockabilly singer Robert Gordon cut a number of Crenshaw's songs. One of those covers, "Someday, Someway," became a minor hit (reaching Number Seventy-four on the pop charts) and helped create a buzz about Crenshaw.

Before long that buzz led to a record deal with Warners Bros. Initially, Crenshaw wanted to produce his own first record, but he later agreed to work with Gottehrer. When Gottehrer suggested session drummer Anton Fig and bassist Will Lee for the sessions, Crenshaw insisted on

sticking with his own group. "I fought to have Robert and Chris on that record," he says, "because we'd forged a group identity and come to that point as a unit."

There were also disagreements over what material to put on the album. "I originally didn't want 'Someday, Someway' on the album," says Crenshaw, "because I felt

Robert Gordon had taken a shot with it already, and I didn't want 'She Can't Dance' on there, since it had been on our Shake single. But I gave in."

Crenshaw and Gottehrer finished the record in five weeks at the Record Plant, in New York City. The final album is an alternately rousing and heartbreaking cycle of infectious pop rockers ("Cynical Girl," "Rockin' Around in N.Y.C.," "She Can't Dance") and ballads ("Mary Anne," "Not for Me") – none of them clocking in at more than 3:07.

Critics loved the album, and it sold well. Crenshaw's single of "Someday, Someway" outperformed Gordon's, peaking at Number Thirty-six.

"At the time, everyone focused on the Fifties-rock influence on my songs," says Crenshaw. "I was widely compared to Buddy Holly – which is a hell of a compliment. But the real influences were bands like Rockpile and Squeeze. I was just trying to do a good day's work." ❖

13

BUILDING THE PERFECT BEAST
Don Henley
Geffen

Producers: *Don Henley*
Danny Kortchmar
and Greg Ladanyi
Released: *November 1984*
Highest chart position: *13*

THE SEVENTIES WERE THE FAVORED habitat of the Eagles, whose tales of "livin' it up at the Hotel California" vaulted the West Coast rockers to superstardom. In the wake of their unannounced breakup around the turn of the decade, the individual members faced the Eighties with a much less certain hold on their audience. While his band mates – especially his erstwhile writing partner, Glenn Frey – have steered a safe, commercial course, Don Henley has written and recorded songs with a sociopolitical conscience, working at a painstaking pace. He has made only three solo albums in this decade.

Building the Perfect Beast is a meticulously crafted and programmed set of songs about love and politics. The first side is given to personal reflections on love and loss, such as the wistful, gorgeous "Boys of Summer." Side two is more issue oriented, tackling subjects from genetic engineering ("Building the Perfect Beast") to America's reckless foreign policy ("All She Wants to Do Is Dance"). The album's longest and most ambitious piece, "Sunset Grill," describes in disturbingly vivid images a character's sense of entrapment in an evil, convulsive metropolis: "You see a lot more meanness in the city/It's the kind that eats you up inside/Hard to come away with anything that feels like dignity."

Henley's collaborator is guitarist Danny Kortchmar, who has also accompanied James Taylor and Jackson Browne. Kortchmar wrote or co-wrote nine of the ten compositions on *Building the Perfect Beast*. The arrangements are more varied and generally edgier than the Eagles' easy-rolling songs – a development consistent with Henley's growing politicization.

"Maybe what I'm trying to do is find a purpose for being in the music business," he told ROLLING STONE in 1985. "I'm trying to make people think a little bit and be aware of things. Maybe rock & roll is not the vehicle for this sort of thing – but I don't see why it *can't* be." ❖

74 SIGN O' THE TIMES
Prince
Warner Bros.

Producer: *Prince*
Released: *March 1987*
Highest chart position: *6*

IT BEGAN AS 'DREAM FACTORY,' A TWO-record set with major contributions from Revolution members Wendy and Lisa, then metamorphosed into *Crystal Ball*, a three-record extravaganza whose lengthy title track was to be Prince's masterwork. But by the time of its release it had once again become a two-disc set, now titled *Sign o' the Times*.

Highlighted by the outstanding Curtis Mayfield-styled title track, one of Prince's strongest social statements, the album is his most diverse work, with material ranging from the steamy funk of "Hot Thing" to more esoteric gems such as "The Ballad of Dorothy Parker" and the fanciful "Starfish and Coffee." This was also the album that marked the return of Prince's more controversial side with the sexually provocative "If I Was Your Girlfriend."

Produced, arranged, composed and performed by Prince, *Sign o' the Times* found him back in complete control of his music. He abandoned the neo-psychedelic qualities that had come to the fore on his previous albums, pursuing a tougher soul music, evident on the title track, "Housequake" and "U Got the Look." "He was hearing a different kind of music," says Alan Leeds, vice-president of Prince's Paisley Park Records.

At first, *Dream Factory* was to have been another band album like the preceding *Purple Rain*, *Around the World in a Day* and *Parade*, but along the way Prince disbanded the Revolution. Instead, he holed up in the basement of his new house and began cutting solo tracks.

Prince played or sang nearly everything on the album, although there were some contributions from Sheila E., former Revolution members Wendy and Lisa and a few others. The three-record *Crystal Ball* concept was followed all the way through to the mastering stage and included a twelve-minute title track. But Prince and Warner Bros. decided a three-record set wasn't the best move, coming after the disappointing sales of *Parade*.

What became the new title track was written toward the end of the recording sessions. "He had begun to see the effect of crack and drugs on young people," says Leeds. "He's not really a preacher, but it's certainly an antidrug song."

"U Got the Look," one of several hits, became a duet featuring Sheena Easton by accident. "Sheena just happened to be around," says engineer Susan Rogers. "He said, 'How'd you like to do this? Feel like singing?' It was very spontaneous."

"If I Was Your Girlfriend" features a very personal lyric, directed at Susannah Melvoin, who had been Prince's girlfriend. "Being Wendy's twin sister, she's very close to Wendy," says Rogers. "It was a way of asking, 'Why can't I have the close-

ness you have with your sister?'"

In retrospect, *Sign o' the Times* looks more and more like Prince's *Exile on Main Street*, one of the few two-disc sets by any artist that holds up through all four sides. "There was a refreshing feeling about making his own music unencumbered [by the band] again," says Leeds. "I think it showed an artist who had really grown." ❧

15 SHE'S SO UNUSUAL
Cyndi Lauper
Portrait / CBS

Producer: *Rick Chertoff*
Executive Producer: *Lennie Petze*
Released: *October 1983*
Highest chart position: *4*

'SHE'S SO UNUSUAL' WAS AN appropriate title for Cyndi Lauper's 1983 debut record: From her electric-orange hair and colorful flea-market wardrobe to her squeaky, giddy voice, Lauper hardly appeared an odds-on bet to become one of pop's premier vocalists.

Nor are many of the songs selected for *She's So Unusual* conventional. "She Bop," a seductive account of female masturbation, "Girls Just Want to Have Fun," an uncut statement about sexual freedom, and "He's So Unusual," a short but sweet taste of a 1929 tune that recalls comedienne Gracie Allen, weren't the kinds of songs that typically add up to a hit album. But that's precisely what *She's So Unusual* became. The multiplatinum disc and its four Top Five singles made Lauper an instant star.

Before embarking on a solo career, Lauper sang with Blue Angel, a group she cofounded in 1978. The band's debut album, released in 1980, bombed, and Blue Angel broke up.

Lauper signed a record deal with Portrait, and with producer Rick Chertoff at the controls she began work on *She's So Unusual*. Chertoff brought in Rob Hyman and Eric Bazilian of the then-unknown Philadelphia band the Hooters to play on the record. Together they opted for a synth-heavy sound that evoked the girl-group era of the early-Sixties and deftly played Lauper's vocals against thick arrangements.

Not yet an accomplished songwriter (although she co-wrote "She Bop" and the touching ballad "Time After Time"), Lauper looked outside for material. She interpreted the Brains' "Money Changes Everything," Prince's "When You Were Mine" and Robert Hazard's "Girls Just Want to Have Fun" with wit and conviction.

That she was able to integrate her zaniness into *She's So Unusual* without sacrificing the underlying seriousness of the songs or her vocal delivery also meant something to Lauper's career. Few solo artists have been able to balance such a delicate dichotomy the first time around. Fewer still have made it seem so easy – and so much fun. ❧

76

SECOND EDITION
Public Image Ltd.
Island

Producer: *Public Image Ltd*
Released: *March 1980*
Highest chart position: *171*

'I DON'T WANT TO LIVE IN HISTORY books," John Lydon told ROLLING STONE in 1979 by way of burying his old band, the Sex Pistols, and praising his new one, Public Image Ltd. "We're trying to write the next chapter." However iconoclastic they had been, the Pistols were "just" a rock & roll band; PiL was an *anti*-rock & roll band, and if the members of the group were on a

search-and-destroy mission, they found their target on *Second Edition*.

Guitarist Keith Levene says the album – which was also known as *Metal Box* because its original U.K. packaging looked like a small film can – represents the peak of early PiL and dismisses the idea that the anarchistic band was all a joke. "It fucking wasn't like that, *okay?*" Levene says. "We were trying to do something serious."

The band wanted a unique album cover and toyed with ideas such as a sardine can that would require a key (not supplied) and even what Levene describes as a "sandpaper-type record, which would fuck up all your other records when you put it in your collection." Eventually, the album was released in the U.K. in a limited edition of 50,000 as three twelve-inch records (recorded at 45 rpm for maximum sonic impact) crammed into an embossed tin can and titled *Metal Box*. The tracks weren't listed on the album or the labels, which were at least color coded. Much to the band's displeasure, the album was released in the United States with a cardboard jacket, a different title (*Second Edition*) and relatively inferior sound.

With Jah Wobble's reggae-drenched bass way up front and Levene's dissonant guitar forays, the band pumps out droning, fragmented dance music –

disco, Samuel Beckett style. Lydon's disembodied monotone vocals sound like they were phoned in long-distance.

Virtually all the songs on the album were improvised in the studio. Bassist Wobble would play until the other two heard something they liked, then structure a track around it, using a clutch of session drummers; Levene says the best work on the record began as mistakes that were then refined and repeated. "There was a great lack of fear, a childlike innocence in the way it was approached," says Wobble.

Many saw in Lydon's lyrics an attempt to bury the Sex Pistols myth (significantly, he had changed his name back from Johnny Rotten). On the opening track, "Albatross," he sings about "getting rid of the albatross," perhaps a reference to former Pistols manager Malcolm McLaren. On "Memories," he wails, "This person's

had enough of useless memories," and "Whatever's past/Could never last."

Second Edition also features three instrumentals, including the beautiful "Radio 4." But according to Levene, dropping vocals wasn't a conceptual statement. "Nobody was around," he says, "and I had to do something with the bloody studio time." ❖

11 ROBBIE ROBERTSON
Robbie Robertson
Geffen

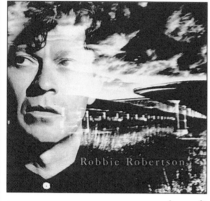

Producers: *Robbie Robertson and Daniel Lanois*
Released: *October 1987*
Highest chart position: *38*

"IT'S EASY TO BE A GENIUS IN YOUR twenties," says Robbie Robertson. "In your forties, it's difficult."

Such was the trepidation with which the former Band guitarist and songwriter approached making his long-put-off solo album. But he needn't have fretted so much: *Robbie Robertson* – released in 1987, a full decade after the Band broke up – is ample proof that Robertson's abilities are still very much intact.

From the album's ethereal opener, "Fallen Angel," dedicated to Robertson's former band mate, the late Richard Manuel, to "Testimony," its hard-rocking conclusion, Robertson establishes himself as his own man. "It was a personal statement," Robertson says of the album. "When I was younger, I thought I was *too* young to really be personal. I thought that what I was feeling and thinking might be half-baked."

Robbie Robertson took three years to complete and cost over $750,000 to make. Traveling to New Orleans, Woodstock, Dublin and England for inspiration and recording sessions, Robertson enlisted the help of U2, Gil Evans, Maria McKee, the BoDeans, Peter Gabriel, two of his cohorts from the Band – Rick Danko and Garth Hudson – and the obscure but gifted guitarist Bill Dillon as sidemen.

Much of the work was done in a studio in Santa Monica that Robertson turned into a kind of workshop-cum-lounge. With guitars and synthesizers at the ready, he spent months and months working on ideas. Although he began the recording sessions with an album's worth of material, many of the songs that showed up on the finished record – "Sonny Got Caught in the Moonlight," "Testimony," "Sweet Fire of Love" and "Somewhere Down the Crazy River" – were written in the studio. "I felt it was important for Robbie to write new songs for this record," says coproducer Daniel Lanois.

Robertson wrote passionately about saving the planet ("Showdown at Big Sky"), the price of fame ("American Roulette") and romance ("Broken Arrow"). "I never wrote about the environment before," says Robertson. "I feel very strongly about this stuff, but [in the past] I felt like I'd be jumping on the bandwagon. Now I felt like I couldn't help it."

Robertson sees the album as just the start of a new kind of songwriting and record making. "I was proud to rip open my chest and bare my soul," he says. "I'm not embarrassed to talk about these things anymore. Do you know what a skin walker is? It's a thing in Indian

mythology. There are certain people born with this gift, and they're able to actually get inside you and mess with your feelings and with your mind. And if a skin walker chooses to get ahold of you, there's not much you can do. I want a song to get inside me, to feel it did the old skin walker on me. I was kind of discovering that on this album, and now I'm pursuing it." ❧

18

DARE
The Human League
A&M

Producers: *Martin Rushent and the Human League*
Released: *February 1982*
Highest chart position: *3*

WHEN THE HUMAN LEAGUE'S AMERICAN debut, *Dare*, began its race up the charts in 1982, both the band and the album seemed unabashed rock rip-offs to more than a few skeptics. The British band, after all, sported no guitars, and there was no drummer or bassist in the group, either. What the Human League used to create *Dare* was a wash of synthesizers performed by band members who didn't even consider themselves to be professional musicians.

"We started out as rank amateurs with a belief that you could use technology to make up for the fact that you hadn't acquired any skill, that you could use computers to make up for the fact that you hadn't any keyboard players, that you could use sequencers to do rhythms rather than employ a drummer," Human League vocalist and songwriter Phil Oakey told *Musician* magazine in 1982.

Dare helped pave the way for the onslaught of electronics that would permeate rock on every level in the Eighties. The album demonstrated that synth pop was a viable alternative to rock's time-tested but guitar-glutted formulas. *Dare* and its smash single, "Don't You Want Me," also proved that the lucrative American market would willingly digest synth pop, provided there was enough in the way of melody and rhythm to overcome the sometimes sterile strains of the synthesizer sound.

Like punk – a movement completely at odds with the kind of pop music a band like the Human League wanted to make – the band confirmed that attitude, and not musicianship, is what's really important in the rock & roll process, and that virtually anyone can play the music.

Produced by Martin Rushent, who had also worked with the Buzzcocks and the Stranglers, *Dare* was Human League's third album. The previous two, *Reproduc-tion* (1979) and *Travelogue* (1980), were U.K.-only releases. Critically acclaimed, both LPs nonetheless possessed largely unfocused attempts at making synth pop an accessible rock style.

After a personnel shake-up in 1980 that left Oakey and Philip Adrian Wright

the only surviving members of the original Human League (Ian Craig Marsh and Martyn Ware went on to form the British Electric Foundation and then Heaven 17), the band was revamped with newcomers Ian Burden and Jo Callis on synthesizers and Joanne Catherall and Susanne Sulley on vocals.

Aside from delivering an alluring synthesizer-soaked brand of rock on *Dare*, Oakey and the rest of Human League further validated their best songs with lyrics that went beyond pop pap. "Seconds," a deceptively haunting song about the JFK assassination, "Darkness," a tune about paranoia, and "The Sound of the Crowd," a satirical stab at conformity, are nearly as memorable as "Don't You Want Me."

But in the end, *Dare* is most remembered for its slick synthesizers, drum machines, dance rhythms and palatable pop.

"We wanted to have a Number One record – like the Beatles," Oakey said. With "Don't You Want Me," the Human League achieved its goal. ◈

79 GUITAR TOWN
Steve Earle
MCA

Producers: *Emory Gordy Jr.*
and Tony Brown
Released: *March 1986*
Highest chart position: *89*

"I HAD GIVEN UP ON EVER GETTING a record deal and became a staff songwriter, going into the office eight hours a day and trying to write for the radio," says the Nashville-based country rocker Steve Earle.

"What happened was that during that period, I learned a lot about craft." When Earle finally did get to make a full-length album in 1986, after having written songs for artists ranging from Waylon Jennings to Carl Perkins, he could apply professional songwriting polish to his Dylanesque verse and outlaw style of music. The result was *Guitar Town*, an album that straddled country and rock to create something startlingly new. In the words of a fellow artist, John Hiatt, it was "pretty much a darn near flawless record. Great writing, fantastic album."

Guitar Town tells simple stories of people living in hard times, such as the cautionary "Good Ol' Boy (Gettin' Tough)." It also relates the autobiographical tale of a country singer rolling down the road, from "Guitar Town" to "Hillbilly Highway," trying to outrun the blues. "It's important to me to make sure the average person can understand what I'm trying to say," says Earle. "Songwriting at its best is very rarely poetry; it's usually narrative and practically journalism. It is a form of literature, but one you can consume while you're driving your car."

Guitar Town boasts everything from a rich, orchestral twelve-string to some deep, twangy solos on the Danelectro six-string bass. It was recorded at an all-digital studio in Nashville. By embracing the latest technology, Earle hoped his hometown would receive its due as an up-to-date music metropolis. "I want to see Nashville become a place to make records, and not just country records," says Earle.

Does Earle see himself as more of a country or a rock artist? "I've been more readily accepted on rock radio, but as my audience gets older with me, I'll probably end up back on country radio," he says. "I think that as a singer, I borrow more from Hank Williams than from David Bowie." ☙

SUZANNE VEGA
Suzanne Vega
A&M

Producers: *Lenny Kaye and Steve Addabbo*
Released: *April 1985*
Highest chart position: *91*

IT WASN'T UNTIL THE RELEASE OF HER second album that Suzanne Vega achieved fame, scoring an unlikely Top Forty hit with "Luka," a song about child abuse. But the singer's 1985 debut album, *Suzanne Vega*, had already awakened listeners to a fresh new voice, reviving the folk-music genre after nearly two decades of dormancy. For Vega, who was then twenty-five years old, the album was cause for uncertainty and isolation as much as triumph. "I felt a little bit like a novelty act," she says.

Vega was certainly an anomaly during the mid-Eighties, softly strumming an acoustic guitar and singing introspective ballads while the rest of the music world was caught up in bigger-is-better events like Live Aid and Bruce Springsteen's *Born in the U.S.A.* mega-tour. In retrospect, however, Vega's intimate first album ushered in a flock of female folk singers, including Tracy Chapman, Melissa Etheridge, Michelle Shocked, Tanita Tikaram and the Indigo Girls.

Having taught herself guitar at the age of eleven, Vega began writing her own songs when she entered her teens. After graduating from Barnard College in 1982, she played small coffeehouses in Greenwich Village – the same area of New York City where nearly every Sixties folkie first tuned up his Gibson. But Vega, a child of the Eighties, hardly fit the protest-singer mold. Even though she carried an acoustic guitar, her hero wasn't folk icon Bob Dylan but punk godfather Lou Reed. There were other differences as well. After years on the Northeastern club circuit, she had developed a direct, emotionally tempered style that she has said was inspired as much by novelist Carson McCullers and painter Edward Hopper as by romantic balladeers.

Weaving these diverse influences into a deeply moving album were producers Lenny Kaye (formerly Patti Smith's guitarist) and Steve Addabbo (Vega's manager), who brought modern touches to Vega's straight-ahead style, enhancing the singer's sparse sound with subtle electric guitars, graceful violins and even New Age synthesizers, all of which added gentle textures to her haunting material.

Vega's prowess with simile and metaphor dominates the entire album, perhaps most effectively on songs like "Undertow," "Freeze Tag" and "Straight Lines." But Vega's sphinxlike wordplay reaches its apex on "Small Blue Thing," a ballad more reflective of an intangible feeling than a literal object. "The song is actually pretty straightforward – it's not a riddle," she says with a laugh. "I never try and be tricky. At the time, I felt like a small blue thing. I never expected that people would think

that it stood for something. Some people even asked if it's a fetus. It's not that at all – it's a mood.

"The structures behind folk music and folk songs are very elemental, sort of like water," Vega adds. "You go through your fads with wine and soft drinks and everything else, but water is the basic thing you always go back to." ❧

1984
Van Halen
Warner Bros.

Producer: *Ted Templeman*
Released: *January 1984*
Highest chart position: *2*

"IT'S REAL OBVIOUS TO ME," SAYS PRO-ducer Ted Templeman when asked why *1984* won Van Halen a broader and larger audience. "Eddie Van Halen discovered the synthesizer."

The foursome had been selling out are-nas for more than a decade on the basis of Eddie's virtuosic, fleet-fingered guitar play-ing, singer David Lee Roth's blunt, raun-chy lyrics and the brute force of Michael Anthony's bass and Alex Van Halen's drums. But *1984*, abetted by tunes that swirled elements of synth pop into metal – most evidently on the hit single "Jump" – and by a string of campy, low-budget vid-eos that found favor on MTV, carried Van Halen to a new plateau of popularity. No longer viewed as threatening to those with a fear of metal, the band somehow be-came amusing and even en-dearing to middle America. And all the while Van Halen continued to rock like crazy.

According to Templeman, who produced all six Van Ha-len albums prior to and includ-ing *1984*, having time to experi-ment in the studio made a difference. "The group was finding out how to do stuff for themselves, rather than 'Here, do this, because we've gotta get back on the road,' " he says. "So they had a little time and got creative. They got into all kinds of different things, because they were bored doing the same old stuff."

At the time, Eddie was in the process of building his own studio with Don Landee, the band's longtime engineer (and now its producer). While boards and tape ma-chines were being installed, the guitarist began fiddling around on synthesizers to pass the time. "There were no presets," says Templeman. "He would just twist off until it sounded right."

One night Eddie and Alex laid down an instrumental demo of what would become "Jump," excitedly ringing up their slum-bering producer when they finished. "I still have it on my answering machine," recalls Templeman with a chuckle. " 'Ted, come on up! It's like three in the morning, but we really came up with something great.' They played a little bit over the phone."

Roth added the lyrics, which he wrote while being chauffeured in his red Mercury convertible, and "Jump" went on to top the charts – heralding the arrival of hard rock and heavy metal in the theretofore impervi-ous Top Forty. "They connected with a pop audience," says Templeman. "What-ever Bon Jovi has today, Van Halen picked up with 'Jump' then."

"Jump" was followed by two more sin-gles from *1984*: "I'll Wait," a ballad whose chorus was written by Roth with an un-credited Michael McDonald, and "Pana-ma," a hard-charging number to which the sounds of Eddie Van Halen's revving Lamborghini were added.

The album turned out to be the last re-

corded by Van Halen in its original con-figuration, as Roth left – not entirely ami-cably – to go solo and was soon replaced by Sammy Hagar. Producer Templeman swears he didn't see it coming: "There were no indicators to signal a breakup at all. Matter of fact, they were really united on that sucker. Balls to the wall, they were going after the world, man!" ❧

82

EAST SIDE STORY
Squeeze
A&M

Producers: *Roger Bechirian, Elvis Costello and Dave Edmunds*
Released: *May 1981*
Highest chart position: *44*

"IN SONGWRITERS GLENN TILBROOK and Chris Difford, the British New Wave has finally found its own John Lennon and Paul McCartney." This statement of high praise for Squeeze's dynamic songwriting duo began ROLLING STONE's review of *East Side Story*, Squeeze's fourth album. Joined by keyboardist and singer Paul Carrack in

his one-album cameo as a Squeeze member, the group filled the album with smart, uptempo pop tunes whose lyrics scanned, in Difford's words, like "suburban short stories."

Difford and Tilbrook credit Elvis Costello, who coproduced most of the album with Roger Bechirian, for providing inspiration and encouraging the band to move into different areas. "Elvis gave us a broader canvas to work on," says Tilbrook. "He considered some songs we'd written that I wouldn't have thought would be Squeeze songs." For example, when Tilbrook was fast-forwarding a tape of demos, he accidentally landed on "Labeled With Love," a country & western number. He hadn't intended to play it for Costello, who nonetheless liked it right away. When Tilbrook protested that it didn't sound like Squeeze, Costello said, "Let's do it anyway."

East Side Story's best-known song is "Tempted," sung in a husky, soulful voice by Paul Carrack, with Costello and Tilbrook chiming in here and there. Difford wrote the lyrics on the way to the airport, and "all the things in there are pretty much all the things that were in my mind on that trip," he says. Though "Tempted" became an FM-radio favorite, it didn't crack the U.S. Top Forty. "It's one of those records everyone thinks is a hit, but it wasn't

really," says Tilbrook. "I was disappointed it didn't do better, but I've felt that way about a lot of our records."

Musical touches both playful and artful, ranging from the surreal, wavering keyboards on "Heaven" to the full

orchestra on "Vanity Fair," adorn *East Side Story*. Yet Squeeze maintains that the record was an uncomplicated one to make. "It was quite an old-fashioned approach to record making," says Tilbrook. "There weren't really any production tricks on it. The production really involved arrangements, and then just a straightforward recording of the songs."

As a side note, the name Lennon cropped up in an unexpected way midway through the sessions. "One morning, Elvis called and said that John Lennon had been killed the night before and that we weren't going to go out to the studio that day," Difford says. "Then he called back and said, 'No, let's just go in, get some drink and play.' We didn't record anything; we were just playing the blues." ❧

83 LET'S DANCE
David Bowie
EMI

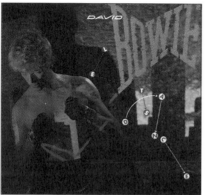

Producers: *David Bowie and Nile Rodgers*
Released: *December 1983*
Highest chart position: *4*

"I WANTED TO COME IN TOUCH WITH the common factor and not seem to be some sort of alien freak," David Bowie told writer Lisa Robinson shortly after the release of *Let's Dance*, his most accessible – and commercially successful – album. "I don't want to seem detached and cold, because I'm not."

A warmer, more open Bowie was evident at every turn on *Let's Dance*, whose bright, upbeat exterior and approachable lyrics celebrate "modern love" and sensual romance beneath "serious moonlight."

Coming off of four hermitic, experimental and disillusioned albums – from *Low* to *Scary Monsters* – Bowie pulled an about-face. His newly found extroversion, complete with a haystack-yellow British-schoolboy haircut, netted him three Top Twenty singles – "Modern Love," "China Girl" and the chart-topping title track. *Let's Dance* was a determined move to recapture the spotlight by a musician who five years earlier had told *Melody Maker*, "I feel incredibly divorced from rock, and it's a genuine striving to be that way."

Let's Dance grafts brassy, big-band swing onto a solid, contemporary R&B foundation. Bowie tapped Nile Rodgers, guitarist for the stylish New York dance band Chic, to produce *Let's Dance*. Excluding Texas blues guitarist Stevie Ray Vaughan, who was Bowie's suggestion, the musicians were drawn from Rodgers's circle. "Except for Bernard Edwards, no person had influenced me more," Rodgers says of Bowie. Yet the collaboration was nothing like what he had had in mind.

"To be honest, when I first got involved, I wanted to do a very noncommercial, avant-garde album," says Rodgers. "I thought I was finally getting a chance to show that black people can do records about things other than dancing, making love and stuff like that. I was quite surprised when I got to Europe and we were working on songs called 'Let's Dance' and 'Modern Love.' " After some discussion, Bowie said, "Nile, I want you to do what you do best – make great commercial records." He trusted Rodgers's instincts, and the album was finished in nineteen days.

Its swift popularity caught the normally unflappable Bowie off guard. "David might not want me to say this," says Rodgers with a chuckle, "but for the first few weeks, even he was surprised. He's a big artist and a rock & roll demigod, but there was still a garage-band guy in there who couldn't believe his record was selling. I'd be lying in bed, and the phone would ring: 'Hello, Nile? This is David. Look what's happening, did you see *Billboard* this week? Wow, unbelievable!' " ❧

84 FAITH
George Michael
Columbia

Producer: *George Michael*
Released: *October 1987*
Highest chart position: *1*

"THERE'S LITTLE THINGS YOU HIDE/AND little things that you show," George Michael sang suggestively on "I Want Your Sex," the incendiary hit that ignited his 1987 album *Faith*. Besides the sensual implications, the lyrics could also describe the British performer's make-over from teen idol to mature pop talent with his solo debut. "I was trying to shake an image – a very glossy, bubblegum image," says

Michael, recalling his early-Eighties career, when he and childhood pal Andrew Ridgeley sang together as the prefab dance duo Wham! After their split in 1985, Michael became intent on finding a fresh start as a solo artist.

Shying away from his persona as a preening dandy who sang drivel like "Wake Me Up Before You Go-Go," Michael cultivated a new approach that was seriously sexy. With torn jeans, perfectly coifed hair and stubble that would make Don Johnson envious, he became the leading progenitor of a style that all but redefined late-Eighties fashion.

But the real change was in the lyrics, not the look. Beyond the beat-crazy dance rhythms, most of the songs on *Faith* revolve around important issues. "I Want Your Sex," for example, raises the issue of monogamy in the age of AIDS; "Look at Your Hands" deals with abused wives; and "Monkey" touches on the horrors of addiction. "I wouldn't have dared approach subjects like wife beating or addiction when I was with Wham!" says Michael. "But I had been liberated from those particular confines."

Michael spent almost two years writing and recording *Faith*, influenced, he says, by "a lot of American radio, which kind of seeped into my consciousness." Months before he began recording the album, he had created "I Want Your Sex" as a song for a friend to sing, but he reclaimed it. "I

Want Your Sex" unleashed a torrent of protest and publicity for the young star. The BBC banned the song in England, and many American stations refused to play it. Nevertheless, spurred by an outrageously erotic video clip and all the surrounding controversy, Michael's sassy come-on sold more than 1 million copies in the United States.

After "I Want Your Sex" scored, the catchy single "Faith" was released in October; the entire album was released a month later. Supercharged by four more hit singles – "Father Figure," "One More Try," "Monkey" and "Kissing a Fool" – the album went on to sell 14 million copies worldwide, and *Faith* became one of the few albums to top the pop and black charts simultaneously. As further evidence of its broad-based appeal, *Faith* subsequently captured a Grammy for album of the year and topped ROLLING STONE's annual readers' poll.

"I was expecting the album to be big, but I wasn't expecting anything like the success it had," says Michael. "There was a fair amount of pressure on me to carve a different niche as a solo artist without actually having to force it. The progression had to be natural, but I also knew there had to *be* a progression." ❧

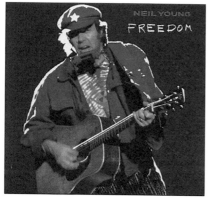

Producers: *Neil Young and Niko Bolas*
Released: *October 1989*
Highest chart position to date: *None*

"I KNEW THAT I WANTED TO MAKE A real album that expressed how I felt," says Neil Young of his most recent album, *Freedom*. "I just wanted to make a Neil Young record per se. Something that was just me, where there was no persona, no image, no distinctive character like the Bluenotes guy or the guy in *Everybody's Rockin'*. It's the first time I've felt like doing an album like this in years."

Freedom veers between folkie ballads ("Ways of Love," "Someday" and "Too Far Gone") and screeching rockers ("Eldorado" and a wild-eyed cover of "On Broadway"). The album is bookended by contrasting versions of the bitter, ironic "Rockin' in the Free World." The opener is live and acoustic, with the audience singing the chorus, while the finale is an angry, electric rendition with an additional verse. (Young used a similar device on *Rust Never Sleeps*.)

"It's the longest album I've ever done," says Young. "It's a real mouthful. When I listen to it, it's almost like listening to the radio – it keeps changing and going from one thing to another."

He'd originally planned to release a purely electric rock album – "Nothing but abrasiveness from beginning to end," he says – that he'd recorded in

New York. (Five songs from those sessions were released on an import EP called *Eldorado*.) For the album that was eventually released, he mixed in material from some subsequent acoustic sessions, looking to strike a balance. The result is Young's most personal and unguarded set of songs in many years.

"Music can be like therapy," he says. "It's like getting parts of yourself out, which I used to do all the time. But I was at a point in my life where I really closed off my emotions about a lot of things I didn't understand. I just shut down the whole program and did things that were more on the surface level, because it was safer. Now I feel time has healed whatever was bothering me so much. I feel more open, and I can write songs that are more directly involved with what I'm thinking." ❧

86

THE RIVER
Bruce Springsteen
Columbia

Producers: *Bruce Springsteen Jon Landau and Steve Van Zandt*
Released: *October 1980*
Highest chart position: *1*

HE WAS A MAJOR ROCK & ROLL STAR. HIS records were FM-radio staples. He sold out coliseums. His live shows were legendary. But by 1980, Bruce Springsteen had not yet placed a single in the Top Twenty, and he hadn't really made an album that fully captured the bracing live sound of the E Street Band.

The River changed all that. The album is the work of a top-notch rock band playing live in the studio. Over the course of two discs, Springsteen displays a little bit of everything that drew people to him. If songs like "Jackson Cage," "Point Blank" and "Independence Day" recall the grim, relentless *Darkness on the Edge of Town,* tunes like the frat rocker "Sherry Darling" and the Number Five hit "Hungry Heart" are lighter and more buoyant. And if the sheer giddiness of "Crush on You" and "I'm a Rocker" make *The River* sound like Springsteen's party record, sobering character sketches like the title track and "Stolen Car" argue otherwise.

The album didn't come easily to Springsteen. "I search for that internal logic that connects everything," he said later. "And if it comes real naturally, it's great. With *The River,* man, forget it. It took many months. *Years,* you know?"

Springsteen remembers that "about ninety songs" were rehearsed and either recorded or rejected. In the spring of 1979, Springsteen and the band began cutting songs like "The Ties That Bind" and "Roulette" (a savage rocker that would remain unreleased for eight years). By that fall, Springsteen and his coproducers, Jon Landau and Steve Van Zandt, had compiled a single-disc album that was to include "Hungry Heart," a rockabilly arrangement of "You Can Look (but You Better Not Touch)" and the still-unreleased gems "Cindy" and "Loose Ends."

But when they returned to the studio after playing two No Nukes concerts in New York, Springsteen decided he didn't want to put the finishing touches on that record. Instead, he was looking for something more expansive – something that would take close to another year to finish.

"I was trying to answer 'Where are these people going now?' " he said. "I had an idea where they were going, but I wasn't really sure. I guess I didn't know where *I* was going, you know?"

On *The River,* Springsteen accepts the fact that contradictions and paradoxes can be part of his music because they're part of everyday experience, and the decision to make a two-record set gave him the space to let his characters go just about everywhere. The trip encompasses a hard-rocking visit to "Cadillac Ranch" and the disquieting vision at the heart of the stark finale, "Wreck on the Highway."

"Bruce Springsteen didn't title his sum-

mational record *The River* for nothing," wrote Paul Nelson in his ROLLING STONE review of the album. "Each song is just a drop in the bucket, and the water in the bucket is drawn from a river that can take you on a fast but invigorating ride, smash you in the rapids, let you float dreamily downstream or carry you relentlessly across some unknown county line." ❧

87

STEEL WHEELS
The Rolling Stones
Rolling Stones / C.B.S.

Producers: *Chris Kimsey*
Mick Jagger and Keith Richards
Released: *August 1989*
Highest chart position: *3*

MOST OF THE SONGS ON 'STEEL WHEELS'
were written by Mick Jagger and Keith
Richards during a three-week session in
Barbados. That get-together was the
make-or-break point for the Rolling
Stones' 1989 reunion – a reunion that had
been imperiled by Jagger's and Richards's
solo records and by a year of public back-

biting between the two.

Their attitudes in approaching the Barbados session say a great deal about the
differences between them. "I said to the
old lady, 'I'm going over to Barbados to
write songs – I'll see you in two weeks or
two days,' " Richards says of the
conversation he had with his
wife, Patti, before leaving. "I
had no idea, and I'm sure Mick
didn't either."

Jagger, however, admits to
having no such doubts about his
ability to work with Richards. "I
never worry about those
things," he says. "I just get on
and do it. Keith is very sensitive
about all that sort of thing. I
said, 'Well, we'll just try. If we
don't do it, we don't do it.' "

Each man brought material
to the session. Jagger had a
rocker, "Hold On to Your Hat," while
Richards had a ballad, "Almost Hear You
Sigh." But they began writing together immediately. "We got two or three songs in
the first hour, and once you get a roll going, there's no problem," Richards says.
"What's good for the music will be good
for us personally."

And Richards says there was something
of a rapprochement. "It was very funny,
because, with all the shit that's been going
down over the last few years, you never
know," he says. "But it was 'Do you remember when you said . . .' and both of us
are cracking up."

Charlie Watts's arrival on the scene
also bolstered Richards's sense of possibili-

ty for *Steel Wheels*. "I drove up to the rehearsal place, and I heard him playing,"
says Richards. "I just sat in the car for five
minutes and listened, and I said, 'Yeah, no
problem. This year's *made*.' "

Musically, Jagger was concerned that
the songs on *Steel Wheels* not repeat the
sort of problems that had made him feel
constrained in the Stones. The album's
most radical departure is "Continental
Drift," with its North African feel and use
of the Master Musicians of Joujouka, from
Morocco. "I never thought I'd get away
with that with the Stones, but they bought
it," Jagger says.

Steel Wheels also seems to have provided Jagger with an opportunity to respond
to Richards's public criticism of him. On
the album's first single, "Mixed Emotions,"
Jagger sings, "Button your lip, baby," and
declares, "You're not the only one with
mixed emotions." But the song ends with
Jagger singing, "Let's stick together." "I

just averted my eyes," Richards says,
laughing, about his response to hearing the
song's lyrics. "Although I realized it's not
'Mixed Emotions,' it's '*Mick's* Emotions.' "

Jagger moans when told of Richards's
remark. "Well, I wrote that about this girl
I know, actually – it's got nothing to do
with the Rolling Stones," he says with a
laugh. "I hate to disillusion you." ❧

LIVES IN THE BALANCE
Jackson Browne
Asylum

Producer: *Jackson Browne*
Released: *February 1986*
Highest chart position: *23*

"AND FROM THE COMFORT OF A dreamer's bed/And the safety of my own head/I went on speaking of the future/While other people fought and bled." With those words from the opening verse of "For America," the first track on *Lives in the Balance*, Jackson Browne turned away from the personal introspection that had characterized his earlier work and took dead aim at one of the most important political issues of the Eighties: U.S. policy in Central America.

The album was inspired, in part, by visits Browne made to Central America in 1984 and 1985, though he had already begun writing "For America" and the title track prior to his trips. "I know that in going to Central America, I was really moved to want to do something," Browne told ROLLING STONE in 1987, "to talk about whether we really believe in freedom and justice for all or if it isn't just freedom and justice for us, while we do the most unspeakable things to other cultures."

Months before the Iran-*contra* scandal broke in the press, Browne sang on "Lives in the Balance" of wanting "to know who the men in the shadows are/I want to hear somebody asking them why." After the arms-for-hostages deals hit the news, the increased public awareness of the U.S. government's covert war in Nicaragua prompted Browne to produce and pay for a video for "Lives in the Balance" well after the album had passed its peak in terms of sales. Discussing the song at the time of the video's release, Browne said, "I imply that the truth is kept from us on a regular basis. I flat out say the government lies. Well, these things are no longer heresy."

Other songs examine related aspects

of the album's political theme. The haunting "Soldier of Plenty" indicts the paternalism of America's attitudes toward its Latin neighbors, while "Lawless Avenues," with touching Spanish lyrics by Jorge Calderón, explores the impact of American foreign policy on life on the home front – specifically, in this case, in the Hispanic ghettos of Los Angeles. And, intriguingly, amid all the hard-hitting sociopolitical commentary stands "In the Shape of a Heart," one of Browne's finest love songs.

Lives in the Balance never achieved the commercial success of some of Browne's earlier records. That hardly mattered to him. "I like this album as much as any I've ever done," Browne said. "And there's a certain comfort, a security that I have, talking about something that I feel this strongly about. And whether or not an album succeeds wildly or not, that's intact." ❧

WHO'S ZOOMIN' WHO?
Aretha Franklin
Arista

Producers: *Aretha Franklin
Narada Michael Walden
and David A. Stewart*
Released: *August 1985*
Highest chart position: *13*

"IF I SEE SOMEONE CUTE," ARETHA Franklin told producer Narada Michael Walden during an initial telephone conversation to discuss working together on an album the singer was planning, "I may wink. Then he may wink, and it's like 'Who's zoomin' *who?*'"

The phrase – which Franklin said was an old New York street expression – immediately caught Walden's imagination. "At that time I hadn't worked on an album by anyone of Aretha's stature," Walden says. "I wanted to design something just for her." The result was the title track of Franklin's 1985 comeback album, *Who's Zoomin' Who?*

The reclusive Franklin had spent many of the preceding years in her hometown of Detroit, looking after her seriously ill father, the Reverend C. L. Franklin. According to Walden, Aretha hadn't sung seriously in two or three years. After her father died in 1984, the singer began thinking about returning to the music scene.

Walden started assembling backing tracks in Los Angeles. Since Franklin doesn't like to travel – she refuses to take airplanes when on tour – Walden brought the session tapes to Detroit, where Franklin added her vocals.

"She had to get reacquainted with being in the studio," Walden says, "and she'd get winded." But it didn't take long for the singer to regain her form. "She'll sing a song down in the lower range maybe four or five times," he says. "Then she'll sing it up in her range and do two or three takes."

Who's Zoomin' Who? produced two

Top Ten singles – Franklin's first album to do so since 1972's *Young, Gifted and Black* – with the title track and "Freeway of Love." The latter boasted a cameo appearance by E Street saxophonist Clarence Clemons. "Sisters Are Doin' It for Themselves" featured Annie Lennox of Eurythmics and was produced by Lennox's band mate, Dave Stewart.

Looking for a male singer to work with Franklin on another duet, "Push," Walden "put out signals, but a lot of people were frightened to death to sing with her." Former J. Geils Band vocalist Peter Wolf, however, jumped at the chance. "Peter's got guts," says Walden. "He put his helmet on and came up in there."

Despite Franklin's awesome reputation as a singer, Walden found her easy to work with. "She's a black Mae West," he says. "She's very fast. I

didn't pull anything out of her. She's so vast and brings so much to her takes that it's more a question of keeping up with her. And when it stops, it *stops*. So you've got to be on your toes. Before any session with her, I'd jog four or five miles just to be mentally alert. You have to be – she's the queen." ❧

...NOTHING LIKE THE SUN
Sting
A&M

Producers: *Neil Dorfsman*
Sting and Bryan Loren
Released: *October 1987*
Highest chart position: *9*

"I DON'T GIVE A FUCK ABOUT ROCK & roll," Sting declared unequivocally in 1987. There was, he complained, "no new fuel in rock music." Instead, he said, musicians should be looking outside of rock to African, jazz and even classical music: "Anything! Anything will do."

. . . *Nothing Like the Sun*, released shortly after that tirade, was *everything* but the

kitchen sink, a double-album banquet of seductive Hispanic and Brazilian rhythms, exultant reggae, big-band jazz and melancholy Euroballadry featuring an all-star, genre-busting crew: Branford Marsalis, Mark Knopfler, Eric Clapton, Rubén Blades and Andy Summers.

Sting's sources ranged from German composer Hans Eisler and Jimi Hendrix (a jazz reading of "Little Wing") to a traditional Chilean courting dance in "They Dance Alone," a haunting tribute to the families of Chile's "disappeared," opponents of the government who are believed to have been murdered. In his lyrics, Sting juxtaposed meditations on death and rebirth – his mother died during the making of the record – with observations on religion, history and, in "Englishman in New York," spiritual and cultural exile.

Literally worlds away from the artful simplicity of his hits with the Police and even his jazz-fusion tangents on *The Dream of the Blue Turtles*, his first solo excursion, . . . *Nothing Like the Sun* is as much a vivid reflection of the mushrooming exploratory fervor among many of Sting's middle-aged pop peers, such as Peter Gabriel, Talking Heads and Paul Simon, as it is an expression of Sting's disgust with the state of pop. Ironically, the eleven original songs on the album were the product not of extensive musical field trips but of five months' concentrated writing in New York City in the winter and early spring of 1987.

"I had already started writing songs before that back in London," he told ROLLING STONE during a Brazilian tour the following year. "But I brought those fragments over. And I had this kind of

monkish life. I lived on my own. I cooked my own food. I went to the gym every day. I took piano lessons. The phone was off the hook. And I worked usually from twelve midday to very late at night." The strict regimen, though, combined with the emotional weight of his mother's recent passing, made it hard for him to be objective about the results. " 'They Dance Alone' was a song I played to people as a demo in my apartment," he says. "People were visibly moved. I was too bound up in it to make judgments."

Sting's record company initially questioned the wisdom of his musical expeditions on . . . *Nothing Like the Sun*. "It wasn't simple enough or directed toward the charts," says Sting. "I said, 'Why underestimate the record-buying public?' " In fact, the album was a commercial success, spawning a hit single in the jaunty "We'll Be Together."

"It confirms my belief that sophistication, or intended sophistication, is not the kiss of death," he said proudly. "As long as you're grounded somewhere in common sense." ❧

91

LYLE LOVETT
Lyle Lovett
MCA 1986

Producers: *Tony Brown and Lyle Lovett*
Released: *April 1986*
Highest chart position: *None*

"THIS IS DEFINITELY AN ALBUM OF the Eighties," says Lyle Lovett, "because it took almost the whole of the Eighties to do it." The line is typical of the dry wit that Lovett employs in his offbeat country and blues songs – and also accurate. Some of the songs on *Lyle Lovett* were written as early as 1979. In 1984, he spent his life savings as well as a loan from his parents to record eighteen demos; ten of these were finally remixed and released in 1986.

The wait paid off. *Lyle Lovett* – an assured, refined collection of tunes about rocky romances, dubious weddings and sturdy old porches – heralded the arrival of a major songwriter who brought absurdity and wit to a field that was normally earnest and predictable.

In 1984, Lovett, a Texas singer-songwriter with a degree in journalism, hooked up with the J. David Sloan band at a music festival in Luxembourg. He returned with the members of the band to their native Arizona, and one day in June, he cut four songs at Chaton Recordings, in Scottsdale. Lovett then drove to Nashville looking for a publishing deal and wound up recording fourteen more demos that August.

He sent the tape around to record companies. They liked the material but wanted him to re-record it, which he refused to do. Finally, the tape found its way to singer-songwriter Guy Clark, who recommended him to Tony Brown at MCA. "When I first heard the demos," says Brown, "I thought, 'How could this tape have been around for more than a week without somebody putting it out?' This guy was so developed, so focused."

Aside from some remixing and minor overdubbing, the tapes were virtually released as is. Brown helped Lovett select ten songs (the rest have appeared on subsequent albums) with an ear to country radio. Four made the C&W Top Twenty.

"I probably would have chosen fewer country songs and weighted it more toward the blues-oriented stuff," Lovett says today. "But it ended up being more representative of my songwriting." And as a homespun sampler of a rookie off the street, it has few peers. ❧

92

FULL MOON FEVER
Tom Petty
MCA

Producers: *Jeff Lynne*
Tom Petty and Mike Campbell
Released: *April 1989*
Highest chart position: *3*

"IT'S ALL IN THE SONGS," SAYS TOM PETTY. "If you've got the songs, it's all very simple. With *Full Moon Fever*, I was lucky in that the songs just kept coming up, and I hit a good period of writing that carried through the Traveling Wilburys."

Full Moon Fever, Petty's first album without the Heartbreakers, fell together almost by accident early in 1988 when he

and new acquaintance Jeff Lynne wrote and cut a few songs together at guitarist Mike Campbell's garage studio. The result was an album of pop nuggets with a bright, Sixties-style sheen.

"I've always loved the British rock and pop of the Sixties, and Jeff feels the same way," Petty says. "Within the Heartbreakers, I represent some portion of that sound, but they have so many other influences. If you take me away from them, this is what you get." The only Heartbreaker involved to any significant degree was Campbell, who coengineered, coproduced and played guitars and keyboards.

Full Moon Fever was truly a garage record. "We actually had to pull the cars out at the start of the day," Petty says, laughing. The sessions were relaxed and unhurried, and Petty credits Lynne, the former leader of ELO, for the upbeat atmosphere. "Jeff just loves to be in the studio," he says. "It's like Disneyland to him: 'All right, we're making a record! Boy, what fun!' And it rubbed off on me and Mike."

The sessions also led to the Traveling Wilburys, the impromptu supergroup whose knockoff album was a sensation in 1988. Roy Orbison began hanging around the studio, and George Harrison showed up to play acoustic guitar on "I Won't Back Down." The idea of four musicians – Petty, Campbell, Lynne and Harrison – strumming around a mike worked so well

it was adapted by the Wilburys.

Petty and Lynne worked up nine songs and then stopped to make the Wilburys record. Afterward, Petty cut three more tracks to round out *Full Moon Fever*, including a "shamelessly faithful" cover of the Byrds' "I'll Feel a Whole Lot Better."

In his lyrics, Petty strove to say more in fewer words, citing Randy Newman's influence. "I'd sung a couple of tracks on his last album, and I was so impressed by his material it made me want to quit the business," Petty says. "He can say so much with a simple line. I just kept thinking I wanted to keep the lyrics real simple, as if it were a conversation."

Some songs were personal, others journalistic. "Zombie Zoo," for instance, was written about a punk club in L.A. following a conversation in a diner with some musicians who played there. "I wrote it as if I were Jed Clampett going to the Zombie Zoo,"

Petty says. "It wasn't meant as a put-down; it was done for comedy's sake." And it caught the spirit of play that marked the sessions. "We did *Full Moon Fever* for the sheer fun of it," Petty says. "We never sweated it. It was the most enjoyable record I've ever worked on." ◊

93

THE NIGHT I FELL IN LOVE
Luther Vandross
Epic

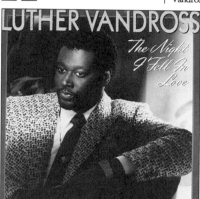

Producers: *Luther Vandross and Marcus Miller*
Released: *February 1985*
Highest chart position: *19*

'THE NIGHT I FELL IN LOVE,' RECORDED IN 1984, was Luther Vandross's fourth album. But this New Yorker with the polished tenor had been in the music business since the early Seventies. He wrote a song for *The Wiz*; sang on, co-wrote and arranged David Bowie's "Young Americans" in 1975; toured as a background singer with Bette Midler, Chaka Khan and Carly Simon; recorded albums as a member of three bands; and did sessions with Barbra Streisand, Quincy Jones and others. He also sang a lot of ad jingles.

But when he recorded his own albums, Vandross says he "got tired of going into the same studios, driving up the same streets and going up the same elevators I had gone up during all my years of sessions. After a few albums, I said, 'There's got to be another way to record.' "

Vandross booked time at AIR Studios, on Montserrat, in the West Indies, bringing with him the same musicians he'd used since *Never Too Much*, his 1981 debut – bassist and coproducer Marcus Miller, keyboardist and arranger Nat Adderley Jr., drummer Yogi Horton and guitarist Doc Powell. He also enlisted Billy Preston on organ and singers Cissy Houston, Alfa Anderson of Chic and Darlene Love.

"We were out of town, so the band wasn't looking at their watches, having a 4:30 Pepsi-Cola jingle they had to go do," says Vandross. "Once you get someone away from that New York session mentality, their whole countenance relaxes and their guard comes down. They take off that bulletproof vest they've been wearing and give you the best that they've got.

"A lot of people go down there because of the comfort," Vandross continues. "There's a cook, there are lots of lounges. It's magnificent. Outside the control room is a big swimming pool on the side of a gigantic mountain that leads to the ocean. The mood it puts you in gives you a better perspective on your music."

Of the album's first single, the finger-popping " 'Til My Baby Comes Home," Vandross says, "That was one of the baddest things on radio. You had a big pop element, without ignoring the soul element." Next was "Creepin'," a Stevie Wonder ballad from *Fulfillingness' First Finale*, followed by "If Only for One Night," a torchy Brenda Russell song Vandross heard Roberta Flack sing on tour.

The moody ballad "Wait for Love," Vandross says, "gets the most applause in concert. We tear that thing up." But the album's most startling song is "My Sensitivity (Gets in the Way)," a romantic's bald confession. "There are only two songs I've written that are *absolutely* personal – 'My Sensitivity' and 'Any Love' [the title track to his most recent album] – and if they apply to anyone else, that's a peripheral consideration."

Discussing the eight tracks on *The Night I Fell in Love*, Vandross says, "Yeah, that's a good album. There was something magical about the way everyone responded to it, which to this day I can't account for." ❧

99 POWER, CORRUPTION & LIES
New Order
Factory

Producer: *New Order*
Released: *March 1983*
Highest chart position: *None*

WHEN NEW ORDER BEGAN RECORDING its second album, *Power, Corruption & Lies* – a landmark album of danceable, post-punk music – late in 1982, it wasn't a band but a mere shadow of Joy Division. Ian Curtis, the Manchester group's singer and songwriter, had hanged himself in May 1980. The remaining members – guitarist Bernard Albrecht, bassist Peter Hook and drummer Stephen Morris – had taken a new name, added Gillian Gilbert on guitar and keyboards and gone back into the studio with producer Martin Hannett.

Movement, New Order's 1981 debut, "owed more to Joy Division than to New Order," Stephen Morris says. The album was recorded "in a situation of complete turmoil," according to Albrecht, the band's reluctant new singer and lyricist. "We were all wondering what to do next." New Order followed *Movement* with a few singles, including "Temptation," a transitional song that incorporated a solid dance beat.

On *Power, Corruption & Lies* – originally released by the British Factory Records in 1983 and reissued in this country on Qwest/Warner Bros. two years later – the band members produced themselves, upgrading from home-built synthesizers and sequencers to state-of-the-art models in the process. "We got the machines two weeks before we went into the studio, and we didn't really know how to work them," Morris says.

"Blue Monday," the first single from those sessions, was "an exercise in learning how to use sequencers," says Morris. "We were trying to create a sort of Frankenstein-monster song, where you just press a button and the song comes out." Released in March 1983, "Blue Monday" is one of the best-selling twelve-inch singles in British history.

The band's struggle with technology helped give *Power, Corruption & Lies* its defining tone, which Morris describes as "fragile and wintery." As is the band's custom, the album's cryptic song titles were added only at the last minute. "Ultraviolence" was a term from *A Clockwork Orange*. The title *Power, Corruption & Lies*, Morris says, came "off the back of a George Orwell book." Peter Savile's cover design shows only a cropped reproduction of *Roses*, by Henri Fantin-Latour, a French impressionist, with no mention of the album title or band name.

A piece tentatively called "KW1" – as in "that Kraftwerk one" – became "Your Silent Face," which offered the first glimpse of New Order's skewed sense of humor. "You've caught me at a bad time," Albrecht sings quietly. "So why don't you piss off." Says Morris, "It was a very majestic piece, and we thought, 'Ah, it's getting too serious.' "

After six weeks in the studio, New

Order went on tour. "We'd recorded these songs but didn't know how to play them," says Morris. "The first night, there was a resounding silence to every song. People just stood there. A lot of hard-core Joy Division fans wondered what we were up to. But fortunately, we started creating New Order songs." ❧

95

SCARECROW
John Cougar Mellencamp
Riva/PolyGram

Producers: *John Cougar Mellencamp and Don Gehman*
Released: *August 1985*
Highest chart position: *2*

"WE WERE BASICALLY IN A PRETTY mean run at that time," says Larry Crane, guitarist with John Cougar Mellencamp's band. "We were going in and getting things done, and the band was clicking."

Scarecrow consolidated the band's rugged, roots-rock thrash and the ongoing maturation of Mellencamp's lyrics. The album is largely about dreams and illusions in America and how the essential character of the nation was being twisted in a government-supported climate of corporate greed. The most visible manifestation of the problem, from Mellencamp's perch in central Indiana, was the rash of farm foreclosures across the Midwest.

Despite the bittersweet, reflective tone of songs like "The Face of the Nation" and "Minutes to Memories" and the sentimental cast of his ode to rural America, "Small Town," the rehearsals that led up to the recording of the songs were nothing but pure fun. The group spent a month, at Mellencamp's insistence, learning a hundred classic rock & roll songs from the Sixties. "We got a bunch of those tapes you see advertised on TV with all the old songs on them," Crane says, chuckling, "and God, we learned everything." They rehearsed behind Mellencamp's house inside what had

been a dog kennel. When a cousin opened up a bar nearby, Mellencamp christened it by playing an entire evening's worth of cover versions, from "White Room" to "Lightnin' Strikes."

When it came time to cut *Scarecrow*, the band members employed the lessons they learned from their Sixties studies. The idea, according to producer Don Gehman, was "to learn all these devices from the past and then use them in a new way with John's arrangements." Mellencamp would make comments like "I want this to be like an Animals record. . . . And I want the overall record to have this kind of a tone, like maybe it was a modern-day Dylan record." Indeed, Dylan himself hadn't been that bitingly topical in years. "You've gotta stand for somethin'/Or you're gonna fall for anything," Mellencamp sings, and on *Scarecrow*, he dug in and made a stand. ❧

96

COLOUR BY NUMBERS
Culture Club
Virgin/Epic

Producer: *Steve Levine*
Released: *October 1983*
Highest chart position: *2*

WHEN TOLD THAT CULTURE CLUB'S 'Colour by Numbers' had been selected as one of the Top 100 albums of the decade, Boy George said, with typical playfulness, "As well it should be."

The band's second LP, *Colour by Numbers* was released in the fall of 1983 while a second British Invasion was dominating the American pop charts. But George insists the album's surprisingly mature pop

polish wasn't motivated by competition with his peers.

"We used to call Duran Duran 'bottles of milk,' they were so white bread," George said. "We certainly weren't competing with Spandau Ballet. We wanted to be more like the older people we admired."

Colour by Numbers does display a respect for pop history. When George debuted the ballad "That's the Way (I'm Only Trying to Help You)" at a sound check one day, he said, "Everyone said, 'Oh, it's really like Elton John.' " After the album was released, George told a reporter that "It's a Miracle" borrowed from the melody of a Gilbert O'Sullivan song. And "Church of the Poison Mind" is nearly identical to Stevie Wonder's "Uptight."

But the familiarity of the group's songs bothered at least one person. "The guy who wrote 'Handy Man' [Jimmy Jones] tried to sue us over 'Karma Chameleon,' " George said. "I might have heard it once, but it certainly wasn't something I sat down and said, 'Yeah, I want to copy this.' We gave him ten pence and an apple."

Culture Club made its second album with the same producer (Steve Levine) and at the same studio (Red Bus Studios, in London) it had used for its debut. George attributes the band's improvement from the tropical pop of *Kissing to Be Clever* to the input of outside musicians, notably keyboardist Phil Pickett, who co-wrote two

songs with the band, and singer Helen Terry, who electrifies several tracks.

Within months of the release of *Colour by Numbers*, George's plucked brow was on the cover of *Newsweek*, followed by a *Tonight Show* bitch-off with Joan Rivers, a Boy George doll and his infamous acceptance speech at the Grammys, when George thanked the audience for "knowing a good drag queen when you see one."

George said he last listened to *Colour by Numbers* three years ago, when he was trying to kick his heroin addiction. "I thought some of the singing was out of tune," he said with a giggle. "It's definitely the best Culture Club album, but I don't know if it's *my* best record." During three recent concerts in Australia, the only song from *Colour* he performed was "Victims," the album-closing ballad. Which doesn't mean he's not proud of the band he may – or may not – be re-forming.

"We had a good formula, and other

groups obviously picked up on that," he said. "I think Wham! definitely picked up on it in the beginning. I've read things where people have said the songs were awful and the only important thing was the way I looked. *Colour by Numbers* definitely does have a place. Above who or below who, I'm not sure." ❧

97
THE MONA LISA'S SISTER
Graham Parker
RCA

Producers: *Graham Parker
and Brinsley Schwarz*
Released: *May 1988*
Highest chart position: *77*

'THE MONA LISA'S SISTER' SIGNALED THE urgent comeback of Graham Parker – an artist who had lost direction following several tough, R&B-fueled albums recorded in the late Seventies. Ambitious and fiercely spare, the album examines the progress of Parker's life in powerful terms, exploring the relative value and meaning of love and loss, work and creativity, success and failure.

"*The Mona Lisa's Sister* was really exciting for me, because I had an idea that was a little off the wall, and I didn't compromise it for anybody," Parker says. "And it paid off." The notion Parker had for his 1988 album was that he should write all the songs and produce them himself – but that proved problematic.

The trouble started when Parker submitted a thirty-song demo tape to his new label, Atlantic Records. The label didn't like the songs and asked Parker to work with an outside producer and collaborate with other songwriters. Parker, who felt that his recent albums had been fatally overproduced, refused. Atlantic released him from his contract, and Parker eventually signed with RCA, where he found the autonomy he craved.

Parker called in guitarist Brinsley Schwarz and bassist Andrew Bodnar, two members of his original backing band, the Rumour. The only other musicians that appear on *The Mona Lisa's Sister* are keyboardist James Hallawell, singer Christie Chapman and drummers Pete Thomas (of the Attractions), Terry Williams and Andy Duncan. The stark, bare-bones production cost a mere $60,000.

The Mona Lisa's Sister is one of Parker's most personal records. The ballad "Success" is a scathing indictment of the ethic that judges people by their material worth. "It was the experience with Atlantic that really kicked the song out of me," Parker says. "Under the Mask of Happiness" takes off from Parker's impressions of Joe McGinniss's book *Fatal Vision* to explore the tensions and denials underlying a seemingly perfect marriage.

The single "Get Started. Start a Fire" – which opens with the lines "The Mona Lisa's sister doesn't smile/She tried to pose but only/For a while" – has an especially personal meaning for Parker. It relates to the album's cover, which depicts a modernist Mona Lisa sporting Parker's trademark shades. "*I'm* the Mona Lisa's sister, you know," says Parker. "And the record company is the Mona Lisa, or something like that. I was the sister who didn't get the painting done of herself."

Looking back at *The Mona Lisa's Sister*, Parker says, "What it's given me is an approach that I can always go back to with the right kind of songs. You can record songs and make them pretty honestly without a circus happening around you and lots of money being thrown away. You really can." ❧

98

LABOUR OF LOVE
UB40
A&M

Producers: *UB40 and*
Ray "Pablo" Falconer
Released: *September 1983*
Highest chart position: *39*

'LABOUR OF LOVE,' BY BRITAIN'S UB40, was exactly that: an enjoyable way of paying tribute to the reggae tunes that meant the most to the band members when they were growing up. The ten numbers they chose to cover from among hundreds they knew and loved were originally recorded between 1969 and 1972 – a period that corresponded to the band members' early exposure to reggae at weekend-long parties in the ethnic neighborhood of Balsall Heath, in their hometown of Birmingham.

In the Sixties, the term *reggae* was used interchangeably with *bluebeat, ska* and *rock steady*. It was Jamaican pop music, meant for dancing. "In those days," read *Labour of Love*'s liner notes, "reggae appealed not to the intellect or the social conscience, but to the heart and hips." Although UB40's own material has often been topical, the group felt that the historical perception of reggae as purely political music was off base, and *Labour of Love* was their way of setting the record straight.

"It's African and calypso rhythms fused together with American rhythm & blues," says guitarist Robin Campbell. "All it's ever been is homemade pop music, and it just gets up my nose when people start talking about reggae as a political or religious music."

The group chose material ranging from the well known (Jimmy Cliff's classic "Many Rivers to Cross") to the unknown (Winston Groovey's "Please Don't Make Me Cry"). UB40's lilting rhythms, uncluttered arrangements and sweet, soulful vocals proved irresistible, and *Labour of Love* helped break UB40, which had been famous in Europe since 1980, in the U.S.

Through a convoluted string of events, "Red Red Wine" – written by Neil Diamond, covered by Tony Tribe and rediscovered by UB40 – became a Number One hit in 1988, four years after its first appearance on *Labour of Love*. The album also reentered the charts, doing better the second time around and outselling the band's then-current release, simply titled *UB40*. "I think it's purely the fact that American radio is now prepared to play reggae, whereas before it wasn't," Campbell says of UB40's long-overdue recognition in the States.

Sax player Brian Travers claims that UB40 may someday do a second volume of reggae covers. "We're going to do another version when we get the chance, just to preserve them," he says. "We do it because the originals are such a turn-on." ◊

99

WHAT UP, DOG?
Was (Not Was)
Chrysalis

Producers: *Don and David Was*
Paul Stavely O'Duffy
and Steve Salas
Released: *September 1988*
Highest chart position: *43*

A DERANGED PAINTING OF A SNARLING pit bull held back on a short leash adorns the cover of *What Up, Dog?*, and a more appropriate image would have been hard to find. Was (Not Was)'s 1988 breakthrough album is an untamed and snap-happy work, a demented, rhythmic blend of classic soul and crazed rock & roll with a bark every bit as ferocious as its bite. And it vindicated the struggling absurdist band from Detroit by proving it capable of commercial success.

Formed by two cynical white songwriter-musicians and fronted by the black vocal duo of Sweet Pea Atkinson and Sir Harry Bowens, Was (Not Was) has always taken a smart, and occasionally smart-ass, approach. "If we had our druthers, we'd be living in a bizarro world where you could make ugly music and earn lots of coal for doing it," says David Weiss, who created the avant-goofball group with childhood friend Don Fagenson.

The band's first two albums had achieved critical raves but miserable sales. Things became so dismal after its second album stiffed that the band came dangerously close to permanent not-was status. With the group in complete disarray, Weiss says he was doing "lamentable" home-video scores, while Fagenson produced "sexual deviants" like transvestite singer Marilyn. Bowen worked with the O'Jays, and Atkinson was "probably watching the soaps and pimping," Weiss says jokingly.

After landing a new record deal in England, the band bounced back with *What Up, Dog?* – a collection of diverse songs ranging from the sentimental and heartfelt "Somewhere in America There's a Street Named After My Dad" to a track about the JFK assassination, "11 MPH." A brilliant collage of musical genres, the album manages to dovetail smooth ballads like "Anytime Lisa" and a calypso-flavored collaboration with Elvis Costello, "Shadow and Jimmy," with more experimental pieces like the primal screamfest "Dad, I'm in Jail." After several of the songs became hits in Europe, the album was picked up for U.S. release by Chrysalis Records.

With so many deliciously wicked numbers, it might seem tough to pick a single highlight, but for Weiss the album's tour de farce is "Wedding Vows in Vegas," a track included on the CD version of *What Up, Dog?* The song is a smoky, sardonic number crooned by cocktail-lounge icon Frank Sinatra Jr. "He came in like a hit man to sing that day," Weiss says of the hour-long session.

After the late-1988 release of *What Up, Dog?*, there was no question which world Was (Not Was) inhabited: "Walk the Dinosaur" climbed into the Top Ten, and "Spy in the House of Love" reached

Number One on the dance charts. But however welcome success may have been, Weiss still sounds like a man with more than a few questions about the merits of pop music. "It's easy to make disgusting, unlistenable records that are just plain weird," he says. "But that's what we do on a good day." ❧

100

SUN CITY
Artists United Against Apartheid
EMI

Producers: *Little Steven and Arthur Baker*
Released: *October 1985*
Highest chart position: *31*

ONE OF THE MOST FERVENT AND FORCE-ful political statements to emerge from Eighties pop music, *Sun City* didn't achieve the sales or wide radio airplay of other cause records like *We Are the World*. Nevertheless, the single and the accompanying album managed to achieve their primary goals: to draw attention to South Africa's racist policy of apartheid and to support a cultural boycott of the country.

"It was completely successful," says *Sun City* organizer and coproducer Steve "Little Steven" Van Zandt, who rallied dozens of top artists to work on the project. "Our goal was to stop performers from going there, and to this day no major artists of any integrity have played Sun City."

A Vegas-style recreational center, Sun City is located in Bophuthatswana, one of South Africa's so-called "homeland" regions where black Zulus were relocated without their consent. In efforts to legitimize the area, Sun City has offered entertainers vast sums to perform there.

Van Zandt wrote the song "Sun City" after hearing Peter Gabriel's "Biko," which eulogizes the murdered South African human-rights activist. But rather than perform it himself, Van Zandt came up with the idea of using artists from various genres to each sing one verse, hoping to break down musical separatism in the United States as well as apartheid in South Africa. More than fifty musicians eventually wound up contributing their talents, including Bruce Springsteen, Jackson Browne, Gil Scott-Heron, Grandmaster Melle Mel, Bonnie Raitt, Lou Reed, Run-D.M.C., Ringo Starr, Pete Townshend and Bobby Womack.

The embarrassment of riches evolved into different versions of "Sun City" for single release and an entire album of outtakes. The album features a jazz track re-uniting Miles Davis with Tony Williams, Ron Carter and Herbie Hancock, as well as Gil Scott-Heron's stark "Let Me See Your I.D." A harrowing glimpse of South Africa's totalitarian regime, which restricts free movement and forces blacks to carry identification papers, the rap song also featured Grandmaster Melle Mel; the Malo-

poets, a South African vocal group; and Peter Garrett, lead singer of Midnight Oil.

Less than forty-eight hours before the album was to be mastered, U2's Bono made a surprise appearance at the studio with a tape of a newly recorded number, "Silver and Gold." Too good to pass up, the song was tacked onto the completed album, although the title never made it on the original cover credits, because the artwork had already been finished. Although the single was never a hit, MTV was willing to air the video, and "Sun City" succeeded in reaching the public.

Several months later, Van Zandt, Baker and others who were involved with the *Sun City* project were able to donate more than a half million dollars to anti-apartheid causes.

"The Sun City project is about informing and motivating people," said a ROLLING STONE review of the album in 1985. "That we can dance while we're organizing is this record's greatest triumph." ❧

Biographies

Michael Azerrad
is a New York-based writer whose work appears regularly in ROLLING STONE and on *MTV News*.

Anthony DeCurtis
is a senior editor at ROLLING STONE, where he edits the record review section. His essay for the Eric Clapton retrospective box set, *Crossroads*, was awarded a Grammy, and he holds a PhD. in American literature from Indiana University.

David Fricke
is a senior writer at ROLLING STONE. He has also written extensively on rock & roll for numerous American and British publications.

Michael Goldberg
is a senior writer at ROLLING STONE. His articles have also appeared in *Esquire*, *Downbeat*, *New Musical Express*, Francis Ford Coppola's much-missed *City of San Francisco* magazine, and several college texts.

Fred Goodman
is a senior editor at ROLLING STONE, where he edits the Rock & Roll section. He is also the author of ROLLING STONE's syndicated weekly album-review column.

David Handelman
is a senior writer at ROLLING STONE. He is a former winner of the ROLLING STONE College Journalism Award.

Jeff Hannusch
is a New Orleans-based freelance writer whose book *I Hear You Knocking* won the American Book Award in 1986.

Steve Pond
has been a ROLLING STONE contributing editor since 1979. He has also contributed to *Premiere*, the *Washington Post*, *Los Angeles Times*, *Playboy* and other publications.

Parke Puterbaugh
is a North Carolina-based journalist and a contributing editor to ROLLING STONE magazine. He is also a coauthor of a series of travel books entitled *Life is a Beach*.

Jeffrey Ressner
is a senior writer at ROLLING STONE. He has also written for *American Film* and *L.A. Style*.

Sheila Rogers
is a senior writer at ROLLING STONE, where she oversees the Random Notes section.

Rob Santelli
is a New Jersey-based music writer. He is currently at work on a book about the New Jersey shore music scene.

Rob Tannenbaum
has been a contributor to ROLLING STONE since 1985, and has also written for *Manhattan Inc.*, the *Village Voice* and *New Musical Express*.

David Wild
is a senior writer at ROLLING STONE and was formerly an editor at *Esquire* magazine.

Special Thanks to:

_____

Sarah Lazin, Jan Borowicz

Tish Hamiltion

Janet Schoenfeld, Jeff Sharp

Tim Reitz, Vinnie Romano

and thanks to all

the record companies whose

albums are

included in this book.

_____